Evolving Models of Language

Papers from the
*Annual Meeting of the British Association for Applied Linguistics
held at the University of Wales, Swansea, September 1996*

Edited by

Ann Ryan and Alison Wray

BRITISH ASSOCIATION FOR APPLIED LINGUISTICS
in association with
MULTILINGUAL MATTERS LTD
Clevedon • Philadelphia • Toronto • Sydney • Johannesburg

British Library Cataloguing in Publication Data

A CIP catalogue record for this book is available from the British Library.

ISBN 1-85359-398-2 (pbk)

Multilingual Matters Ltd

UK: Frankfurt Lodge, Clevedon Hall, Victoria Road, Clevedon, England BS21 7HH.
USA: 1900 Frost Road, Suite 101, Bristol, PA 19007, USA.
Canada: OISE, 712 Gordon Baker Road, Toronto, Ontario, Canada M2H 3RT.
Australia: PO Box 586, Artamon NSW 2064, Australia.
South Africa: PO Box 1080, Northcliffe 2115, Johannesburg, South Africa.

Typeset by Wayside Books, Clevedon.
Printed and bound in Great Britain by Short Run Press, Exeter.

Contents

Introduction

ANN RYAN and ALISON WRAY
University of Wales, Swansea

Evolving Models of Language, the deliberately ambiguous theme title for the 1996 BAAL Annual meeting, offered an opportunity for different interpretations, including *models of language that evolve, how models of language are developed* and *models of how language evolves*. Papers taking all three of these perspectives were forthcoming, and many stimulating discussions resulted.

Models in applied linguistics can operate at four major levels: language processing, language learning, linguistic analysis and language testing. Each of these levels is the focus of at least one paper in this collection and in several it is possible to see how interdependent these four levels are.

Two papers focus on practical issues in language testing. Malvern & Richards provide a solution to a weakness inherent in the calculation of lexical diversity in the output of learners and the language impaired. The Type-Token-Ratio (TTR) calculation and its many variations either suffer from unavoidable weightings of the score according to other variables, including the size of the sample and the length of individual utterances within the sample, or, conversely, they are limited by calculations that do not allow the full dataset to be exploited. Malvern & Richards' solution is a procedure which uses increasingly large samples from the data to match the profile predicted by the model to the individual's actual performance.

Milton & Hales also tackle an empirical problem head-on. They are interested in assessing the extent to which text *difficulty* (for L2 learners) is independent of text *technicality*. Using a model of difficulty based on the distribution of frequent and infrequent words, they are able to demonstrate that their technical text, the Nissan car technical manual, is both difficult and also, independently, technical, displaying lexical and grammatical features that cannot be picked up by word-frequency counts. They conclude that a diagnostic for text technicality needs to be based on a model with specific additional features.

Charles Alderson's paper is a critical evaluation of Pit Corder's and others' models of language learning. He argues that formal, external models are of only limited value, and that more account needs to be taken of the internal models of the learners and teachers (whether explicit or implicit), as these will inevitably filter or distort the way in which any external model is interpreted and applied. He warns that linguists may make assumptions about language teaching and learning that are borne of their own enthusiasms and perspective, neither of which are necessarily shared by the average learner or teacher.

Nick Ellis' model of language acquisition and learning challenges the very heart of the Chomskian account of processing, namely, that language is the product of somewhat complex innate mechanisms. Rather, he argues, 'its complexity emerges from simple developmental processes being exposed to a massive and complex environment'. Not only does this paper present an alternative account for how language 'evolves' in the individual, and with significant implications for its actual evolution in our species, it is also a significant contribution to the current evolution of linguists' models of language. These are identifying many of the weaknesses inherent in the Chomskian paradigm that has been dominant in linguistics for so long, and are creating accounts of language processing and learning that are fundamentally different in kind.

Mike Stubbs challenges the integrity and systematicity of Critical Discourse Analysis (CDA) as currently practised, arguing that there is an inherent subjectivity and circularity which could be avoided by using tools such as corpus analysis to demonstrate and justify its claims. He is thus proposing a substantive addition to this analytical model, changing its nature from purely qualitative to qualitative and quantitative.

The remaining two papers in this collection represent the many in the conference itself that were independent of the annual theme. It has always been BAAL's policy to select the best papers on offer, using the theme as a focus but not a strait-jacket, and acknowledging that important research should be presented irrespective of whether it happens to coincide with the chosen theme. Both the papers included here relate to the analysis of academic writing, but in quite different ways. Okamura's study of politeness and hedging in academic articles, supported by interviews with the writers about their intentions and attitudes, reveals subtleties in the relationship between the academic writer and his expert audience. Charteris-Black reports on the use of punctuation by native and non-native speakers of English, and demonstrates that it is the Malay and Chinese learners, rather than the native speakers, who provide the closest match to the prescriptive model.

Linguistics is not an old enough discipline to have developed too many traditions and ingrained paradigms. Symptomatic of a comparatively young field is that its models can be fundamentally challenged and that they can be seen to change and develop – to evolve – within a relatively short time. Linguistics is dependent for its methodology and analyses on a range of other disciplines. Its strength must lie in its ability to draw swiftly on the newest and the best from each of them, using them to create new insights and methods that can rapidly enhance our understanding of the processes of language and provide ever better ways for us to engage in the practical tasks of *applied* linguistics, in its widest sense.

1 Models of Language? Whose? What For? What Use?
BAAL 1996 Pit Corder memorial lecture

J. CHARLES ALDERSON
University of Lancaster

Introduction

In this paper, I present a critical stance towards some of the views of Pit Corder, not in order to belittle the significance of his work and his achievements, which are many and well recognised, but in order to problematise the role of language in language teaching with the benefit of 25 years and more of hindsight, experience, and developments in the field of language teaching and applied linguistics. I shall argue that the view of linguists and applied linguists that up-to-date models of language must be at the core of language education and language assessment is naive, misguided and lacks empirical support.

Corder's stance on the role of models of language is well known. A typical statement reads as follows:

> Linguistic knowledge, that is, knowledge about language in general, and about a specific language, and consequently the ability to talk about it, has always been fundamental to language teaching. It has been, to a considerable extent, taken for granted, since it has always formed part of the normal education of an educated man in advanced societies. It is not possible to imagine that any systematic preparation of materials for teaching could be undertaken without it, unless we restrict what we mean by language teaching simply to the activities of the teacher with the textbook in his hand. (Corder, 1973: 284)

This view is not necessarily shared by learners themselves, however. Consider the following anecdote. A colleague of mine, an engineer, once told me that he was taking yet another French course: he had done evening classes, Languages for All courses and weekend special intensive courses over a number of years, with little success or progress. Yet he was now planning to take yet another evening class. When I asked him why, he said he simply wanted to learn to speak French on holidays. When I questioned his reasons for persistence in the face of apparent failure, he replied: 'I'm looking for a teacher who will teach me how to speak French. So far all the teachers I've had have insisted on teaching me the grammar. I'm not interested in the grammar, I just want to speak the language. The problem with all these language teachers is that they are interested in grammar and the way the language works. I'm not, I just want to speak French.'

For some learners, at least, the role of 'grammar' is less important than it appears to be to teachers.

Many university modern language teachers bemoan the 'fact' that their students do not have any metalanguage. It is claimed that students do not 'even' know what an adverb is. (See Alderson, Clapham & Steel, 1995 for an account of such beliefs.) Apart from the fact that many *linguists* have difficulty saying what an adverb is, one possible reaction to such complaints is to question the need for metalinguistic knowledge, whatever the facts are about actual levels of knowledge. If students simply need metalinguistic knowledge in order to understand language classes because such metalanguage is in common use, one possible option is to change the way one teaches, and avoid using metalanguage. Such suggestions are, however, frequently met with blank looks, and, after some reflection, the assertion that students need to learn metalanguage anyway, since many will go on to become teachers. The assumption that teachers need to have metalanguage goes unchallenged.

In short, language teachers are interested in language and expect learners to be, and they assume that knowledge about language, based on models of language, is useful and relevant to language teaching and learning. However, this view is open to question on a number of grounds, which will form the body of this paper.

Which Model of Language?

Models of language have changed considerably over time, especially in the past 30 years or so. However, whilst it may be a truism to say that language is very complex, one implication of this complexity is that inevitably no one model can be comprehensive or even inclusive and others will always add something.

It is probably also true that no one model is hopelessly inadequate: Chomsky's derision of structuralists has not devalued their work or indeed their methods. One can argue that corpus linguistics enables us to do what Bloomfield simply could not because he did not have the technology. Empirical data collection and description are now commonplace, through the use of electronic corpora, despite Chomsky's criticism of the derivation of theories of language from language data, on principle. Applied linguists are thus faced with many models of language, some claiming to be radically different, some perhaps not really so different, and the possibility exists that different models can complement each other. How far from 'language' can our models of language go in our present preoccupations with communication in social settings, before they are no longer models of language?

McNamara (1996) recounts an anecdote which nicely illustrates the problems applied linguists face when they try to develop assessment measures based on models of language as communication.

> In the design of the Occupational English Test, I wanted the candidate to take part in simulations of clinical communication, particularly with patients. When I investigated further, I found that this was precisely what was done in the teaching and assessment of clinical communication skills for native speaker health professionals in various training contexts. I naturally went to observe these role play assessments. What I discovered was that the focus of the assessments, and the criteria for successful performance, were profoundly different from those I was familiar with in second language testing. In the communication skills assessment of native speakers, silence and economy of contribution where appropriate were rewarded (in the interest of allowing room for the patient to speak); I know of no second language speaking test where this would be encouraged. Similarly, for the native speakers, effective communication was seen as requiring the integration of professional knowledge and psychological presence of mind in the communication; the very thing that second language testing contexts seek at best to control for, at worst to exclude. No wonder that one of the medical educators I spoke to finally got the point when I discussed my preoccupations with her: *Oh, so you're only interested in language, not communication.* (1996: 8)

If the question *whose model are we to use?* is virtually impossible to answer in any reasoned way, at least we can explore the models that are used by applied linguists and what evidence there might be that the model chosen makes a substantial difference.

The development of the Common European Framework is going to be fairly influential in language assessment and teaching over the next few years, especially in continental Europe, and so presumably it matters what model or models are used as the basis for the Framework. The intention is 'to develop a Common European Framework for the design of courses, materials and syllabuses for language learning, teaching and assessment.' (Trim, 1996). It clearly represents an important undertaking and embodies a massive hypothesis about the nature of language and how it is to be operationalised.

To quote again:

> The Framework is based on an analysis of language use and the language user in terms of the strategies employed by users (including learners) to activate general and more strictly communicative competences in order to carry out the activities and execute the processes involved in the production and reception of texts dealing with particular themes, so as to be able to fulfil the tasks facing them in the situations arising in the various domains of social existence. (*op cit.*)

This is a massive and potentially highly influential undertaking, much as were the Council of Europe sponsored developments of Waystage, Threshold, Mastery and other 'levels'. Presumably, the model on which such a Framework is based is important. If the model is ill-informed, or superseded, work based on it will be devalued. That, at least, would be a reasonable inference from the Corder view of the role of a language model.

However, in what follows, I shall argue that the choice of model may be less important than the need to take account of the implicit (rather than explicit) models of language of those who teach, test and learn language. I shall assert that such implicit models will influence both how those involved react to new models and how they learn or do not learn. I shall argue for a research programme that will investigate this assertion, and help us better understand what models of language are held by participants in language education, and what influence and value they have.

What is the Purpose of a Model of Language?

For a linguist as well as an applied linguist, the answer to this question may be self evident: to discover the Truth about language, for its own sake. Models of language help us understand the nature of language better, help us to understand what distinguishes us human beings from the rest of the animal kingdom.

Katz & Fodor's (1963) view is not untypical: 'The goal of a theory of a particular language must be explication of the abilities and skills involved in the linguistic performance of a fluent native speaker' (1963: 181).

Applied linguists may be expected to have professional reasons for developing better, more adequate models of language: since language is what we are supposed to know about, and since language is the centre if not the focus of our professional lives, it would surely be odd if we did not know as much as possible about language. Applied linguists are, after all, interested in language: that is why they do what they do.

Models of language almost certainly underlie what we do as applied linguists anyway, implicitly if not explicitly, and therefore in order to improve our professional activities, perhaps we need to understand more explicitly what models they are based on. I shall take language testing as an illustration of how models are used explicitly or implicitly in applied linguistics.

A test needs construct validity: it needs to be based on an appropriate view of language. It is impossible to develop or even think about developing a language test without some notion of what it means to know, learn, use a language. If we decide to test grammar, we must have assumed that grammar is important, that we know what we mean by grammar, that we can identify it when we see it, that we can characterise grammatical ability, and so on. This does not imply discrete-point approaches: we can make judgements about accuracy in a person's linguistic performance without developing individual test items (and indeed without developing language tests: as humans we judge language all the time, and those judgements will be based on what we think language is and how it is appropriate to use it).

Some testers have therefore developed explicit models of language ability in order to base their tests on them: the most influential of these, the Bachman model (Bachman, 1990) derives from Hymes and Canale & Swain. The advantage of having an explicit model like the Bachman model is that it can be studied, criticised, its implications understood, its assumptions questioned, and it can then be improved. However, a model needs to be empirically tested: not just criticised speculatively. Bachman's model has been much referred to, but little operationalised, to date.

A cautionary tale is in order, with regard to the use of the latest models of language for language test construction. B. J. Carroll & colleagues developed the original ELTS test by explicit reference to Munby's model of the Communicative Needs Processor (Munby, 1978). This model was fairly influential in syllabus and test design in the late 1970s, despite the fact that it had been heavily criticised. Carroll *et al.* were also criticised for using a non-empirical approach to the application of the model in the development of test specifications and later test development. (Note that this is not an inherent critique of the model, since Weir (1983) appears to have implemented it successfully in his development of the TEEP test.) I would argue, despite such criticisms, that Carroll was doing what good applied linguists should do and what Corder advocated: he used what he thought was the best and most appropriate model available.

Unfortunately, time passed, fashions changed, and by 1986 (less than a decade after the introduction of the Munby-based ELTS test), it was felt that the

Munby model was out-of-date, and that the ELTS test needed to be adjusted to take account of more recent thinking in applied linguistics. (There were other more practical reasons for the adjustment also, that had to do with practical issues like test cost, test length, test complexity and so on, but they are largely irrelevant to this cautionary tale.) Caroline Clapham and I were charged with the task of directing the ELTS Revision Project, and therefore one of the first things we did was to consult with applied linguists to see what models had superseded the Munby model on which we should now base the revision of the ELTS test.

Alderson & Clapham (1992) report our failure to identify any consensus on an appropriate model. Many of the suggestions made related to individual aspects of language (e.g. the role of a model of grammar in language ability) or to the particular interest of individuals (e.g. the suggestion that we incorporate some test of aptitude or cultural adaptability). Were we to wait for consensus on a better model? Clearly we had no choice but to continue. As a result, the revised test was not based on an explicit model of language, although a study of the test specifications would doubtless reveal some eclectic model bearing some relation to a communicative view of language use.

The criteria for assessment of language performance developed in parallel with language tests often reveal interesting insights into implicit models of language and also of language development. The well-known FSI/ASLPR scales make explicit statements about development.

Even when scales are not so extensively developed as these, the use of scale categories or rating criteria like 'accuracy' and 'fluency' assumes that such 'things' exist and can be judged. It might be argued that descriptions in rating scales are only as good as the theory of language on which they are based. But is this true? Are such scales in fact based on theory? Fulcher (1993) develops an empirical methodology for scale development that depends upon linguistic descriptions of features of candidates' performance, statistical treatment of the data to see which features relate most closely to proficient performance, and a heuristic for deriving scales from such analyses. Scales need not simply be developed from armchair speculation and intuited notions of the nature of proficiency.

Another common method for deriving scales is for 'experts' to examine performances of typical candidates, to comment on features that are salient for them, and for scales to derive from compilations of these comments. Such a procedure depends upon the experts' perceptions, which may well be based on an implicit theory, rather than an explicit theory.

An important issue is how such scales are used. The use of rating scales depends upon human raters making judgements, and such judgements may or may not relate directly to what is described in the scales. Rater training is a common procedure in language testing, in an attempt to ensure reliability of scores, but in many settings (for example, UK university foreign language departments) such training is still rare. Esser (1995) and Horak (1996) have shown how different participants in the rating process have quite different perceptions of fluency in German (Esser) or proficiency in French (Horak), deriving without doubt from somewhat different views of what is important in proficient language performance – different implicit models of language.

Even with careful training, we cannot be sure that raters are not actually using their own internal models (values/prejudices) when rating – especially when one of the criteria is a term like 'fluency', which is notoriously variable even in its linguistic definitions, and whose lay meaning may very well override any verbal definition given in scale descriptors.

What I have illustrated with the example of language testing could equally have been shown in other areas of applied linguistics. Language testing is not a special case, nor are language testers worse than other applied linguists at selecting, operationalising or interpreting their models of language. They are probably simply more explicit about what they do. The important point is that models of language are pervasive in language testing even if they are implicit. In what follows I shall confine myself to language teaching broadly conceived: textbooks, tests, classroom behaviours and stated beliefs. However, what I have to say about implicit models can be applied, mutatis mutandis, to other areas of applied linguistics, precisely because we ALL have views of language by virtue of the fact that we are all language users.

Views on the Role of Models of Language in Language Teaching

Corder himself was quite clear:

> What I wish to suggest is that a teacher cannot teach a language by any of the current techniques without linguistic knowledge, and that he does make constant use of what are basically linguistic concepts in his teaching. Indeed the suggestion that a teacher can manage adequately without the sort of knowledge I have outlined, however vague, confused and unsystematic, is preposterous. Since trained teachers do invariably use linguistic notions in their teaching, whether they realise it or not, it is clearly desirable that as far as possible these should be the best available and because of the great amount of research devoted to language in recent years this means the most recent. (1973: 276)

My view is that this is considerably overstated, for the following reasons:

(1) The most recent research may be the most irrelevant or the most opaque.

(2) There may well be a difference between what teachers know – or say they know – and what they do in class. What they do may be more important, not only in terms of the rules they give, but what they choose to focus on in error correction, how they give feedback on performance, what they ignore and don't praise, and so on.

The use of a theory of language is at least in part to enable language description:

> The starting point of every application of linguistics to any of the practical tasks is a description of the language or languages involved in the task. The possession of an adequate description of natural languages is a prerequisite for the most efficient carrying out of these tasks and is common to all uses of linguistic knowledge in practical affairs. In the case of language teaching it is true to say that we cannot teach systematically what we cannot describe. (Corder, 1975: 5)

This is something of an overstatement: it privileges explicit description over other forms of knowledge, and other bases for action. However, the real problem is practicality. Do we have to wait for a complete and adequate description, whatever that might be, before we can engage in successful, or even systematic, language teaching? That would be absurd.

Corder fortunately qualifies what he has asserted: 'Our ability at the present time to describe a language from any of the various theoretical points of view is still severely limited and yet learners do succeed to a large extent in learning languages.' (1975: 5). Indeed:

> It is a characteristic of applied linguistics that the practical problems with which it attempts to deal can rarely if ever be solved by reference to one theoretical approach to language alone. (1975: 6)

This advocacy of ecleticism is typical, both of Corder and of Edinburgh in the 1960s and 1970s. It is justified by its purpose, which is other than developing a theoretically pure model. However, one must wonder what the status is of any model of language which is based upon ecleticism.

But, are teachers really so dependent on the latest and most complete theories and descriptions? If Universal Grammar and parameter setting are current notions in linguistics, must teachers incorporate these into their theory of language learning and modify their practice? Why? What gives a linguist or even an applied linguist the right to say that teachers need to know this or that, that teachers' models of language are outdated and they need – Language Awareness? an understanding of UG? to study Critical Discourse Analysis?

Of course, what gives some people the right is their position of authority: they are 'experts' in language: they have devoted their lives to it, and therefore they are 'authorised': they have the power. Perhaps critical discourse analysts should look at the use and abuse of such powerful positions among our own community, and examine how people use language in order to persuade others of the rightness of their particular views of language: What assumptions lie behind the words? What discourse tricks are used in the articulate pleadings? What evidence is appealed to to justify the claims? Above all, how do we claim the right to tell practitioners what they need to know?

For Corder, language and the theory of language are clearly at the core of applied linguistics, and much is made of the need for adequate, complete, comprehensive and theoretically grounded descriptions, despite the admitted fact that none have ever been achieved. Do we have here a case of an overstated need for explicit models and descriptions of language? What *is* the relevance and role of linguistic theory and language description? and where do the learners' and teachers' perceptions and implicit theories come in? How are they mediated and do they mediate?

> If linguistic knowledge had no relevance to, or use in, language teaching, then potentially any native English speaker who had general teaching ability and nothing more could teach his own language. Any such person could walk into a classroom and start teaching English ... Merely to state the proposition in this form is to show its absurdity. (Corder, 1973: 278).

Would that this were true. The existence of schemes like the Japanese English Teachers scheme, or the activities of the Peace Corps and VSO in Africa and East Europe, or the use of native-speaker untrained teachers in Southern Europe, all strongly suggest that, however absurd, it is not uncommon.

Corder's view is both static and unidirectional: applied linguists develop a language description which is applied to the creation of syllabi, textbooks and maybe even classroom procedures. It comes from the expert and needs to be understood by the teacher. Leaving aside the issue of the implicit (or explicit) power relations between applied linguist and teacher, such a view appears to ignore what teachers already know, although we shall see later that Corder does indeed recognise that teachers have implicit ideas about language.

> It is because of the indirectness of the relation between the insights that theoretical studies of language yield and the practical preoccupations of the classroom that many teachers have failed to see the relevance of linguistic studies to language teaching. (Corder, 1975: 5)

This seems to imply that it is the teacher who fails, not the applied linguist. But why should we blame the teacher, and not the applied linguist who has failed to demonstrate 'the relevance of linguistic studies' and failed to apply the theories and models convincingly and practically? It is surely at least arguable that the applied linguist has not taken account of the teacher's (and the student's) implicit theories, and has all too often simply asserted the relevance of the latest theory. Van Lier (1992) points out that very often linguistics is poorly taught, in transmissive mode: that can hardly help to encourage teachers to adjust their models of language, as we discuss below.

Teachers' Implicit Models

In summary of the argument so far, pronouncements of the sort I have quoted above are problematic, not only because of the implicit assumption that models should be handed down to teachers, but also for the apparent belief that teachers do not have models of language available to them. In fact, Corder did not believe that teachers are 'empty vessels' waiting to be filled with the latest linguistic models. Having likened practical language teaching to baking a cake (!), Corder writes:

> Good language teachers do not work by rule of thumb or recipe. They possess, like good cooks, a set of principles which guide their work, in other words, some general notions about what is going on when people learn languages, an informal 'theory' about how languages are taught and learned. I call it an informal theory because, while experienced teachers certainly do possess such general principles, they may not be able, or may not have tried, to formulate them explicitly and clearly in words ... But it is only when principles are explicitly formulated that one can evaluate them or test them in order to see whether they might, in parts, be mutually contradictory and whether they are sufficiently comprehensive and detailed to provide a basis for solving the many different kinds of problems that arise in the course of the teacher's professional work. (1975: 1)

He continues:

> To have some general principles is clearly better than having none, and to formulate these principles is more useful than leaving them implicit because then at least one can set about examining them systematically in order to evaluate them. (1975: 1)

> The linguistic knowledge of most teachers derives from the theories current half a century or more ago, and nowadays often called traditional ... Most teachers will agree from their own experience in the classroom that their (philological studies) (if they did any) have not been of great direct help to them in their teaching. (1973: 276)

One is forced to wonder whether the same could be said of Transformational, Universal or even Systemic Grammar.

> It is at least partly the fault of the academic linguists that so little of the advances in their discipline in this century have found their way into the syllabuses of schools, colleges and university language departments ... There are hopeful signs that this situation is being put right, and a number of universities are now including courses in general linguistics for their students of languages both foreign and mother tongue. (1973: 277)

This appears to imply that what language teachers need is a good dose of current linguistics, and ignores matters like the nature of such courses, how relevant they are or indeed can be, and how they are received by students.

Corder's position seems to be that all that teachers need is better models. Indeed, this is a common assumption of the current Language Awareness movement as well and not just of academic linguists and applied linguists. Brumfit *et al.* (1996) recommend a dose of Language Awareness for the teachers whose classes they observe and describe. Behind such assertions lurks a naive innovation theory: *expose the teachers to the Truth and their behaviour will change.*

There are lessons to be learned from studies of the supposed existence of washback of tests on teaching. The notion that tests have influence on teaching is very commonplace, but almost completely unresearched (Alderson & Wall, 1993). This influence is usually held to be negative, although some writers have suggested that washback can be positive if the test is a good test. It was in order to investigate and establish the existence of positive washback that we carried out a study of the effects of introducing an innovative school-leaving examination in Sri Lanka. To our surprise, we discovered that although teachers were observed to be influenced in what they taught by the content, or at least the supposed content, of the examination, there was much less impact on the way they taught: there was considerable evidence (reported in Wall & Alderson, 1993) that teachers did not change their teaching methodology from that observed during baseline studies. This finding rather surprised us, and we were forced to revise what we now see as a naive view of how things can change.

Wall (1996) explores how tests might be introduced into traditional systems by looking at innovation theory outside language education, in general education. In particular, she refers to Fullan (1991).

Wall gives examples of the questions Fullan suggests be asked during the initiation phase of an innovation:

> Would-be innovators should ask themselves questions like the following:

> Where did the idea for change come from? From a teacher, or a group of teachers? From an academic? From a politician?

What was the motivation behind the idea? Was it to solve a problem which practitioners agreed needed solving? To test out a theory? Or to take advantage of opportune funding? What do these different motivations suggest about the long-term commitment of the initiator?

What can be said about the 'quality' of the innovation? Has the idea been well thought through? Is it clearly described? Is it specific enough without being too prescriptive?

Do teachers have access to information that will help them to understand the idea or begin to implement it? Or is this information available only to its originators (who are sometimes academics out of touch with the classroom)?

Who in the establishment will support the idea? Will they have enough influence to get it adopted? Will teachers support the idea? What conditions must be there to convince them that it is practical and helpful?

Are external change agents involved in any way? What role should they play?

(Wall, 1996: 339)

Wall concludes that the content and methods of the examination itself are of relatively minor importance to the success of innovation through testing compared with other factors. Thus, whilst content and method are crucial to test validity, the success of the innovation does not depend on the validity of the test.

There are important lessons for language education in general from this paper. In particular, simply presenting teachers with a 'better' model of language (even if it is called Language Awareness, and is delivered with an appropriate methodology, as van Lier advocates) will not ensure, and may not even relate to, changed classroom practice.

Textbooks

A textbook embodies the major part of the linguistic contribution to language teaching. (Corder, 1973: 278)

Although the analysis of textbooks from various angles is fairly common, especially as part of teacher training courses, it is naive to assume that because a textbook embodies a particular theory of language, the resulting language teaching will also reflect such a theory. Research into aspects of the use that is actually made in class of textbooks is rare in language education. Bonkowski (1995) shows how teachers either ignore the teachers' guides to textbooks, or make selections from the text and the teachers' guides and distort the authors' intentions. In short, teachers interpret the intentions of the author through their own models, not only of language, but of language learning and language teaching. To assert, therefore, that textbooks embody the major contribution of linguistics does not necessarily tell us much about the contribution of linguistics to language teaching as it is experienced by language learners. Bonkowski's study is important in that it demonstrates a number of the factors that influence how teachers interpret and implement textbooks and their models, and it emphasises the importance of *not* assuming that all we need to do with our models of language is to ensure that they are incorporated into textbooks and syllabuses (and examinations).

Learners' Models and Error Analysis

In this paper so far, I have concentrated on teachers and materials, be they textbooks or tests, as being important containers of models of language. But what about the learner's models of language? In fact, there appears to be very little literature on this, other than the Second Language Acquisition literature on grammaticality judgements. However, this field tends to be prescriptive, in that it makes judgements about the quality of the learners' metalinguistic knowledge, rather than exploring its nature for what it can reveal about the state of that knowledge and its possible influence on learning. The risk is a simplistic (unfavourable) comparison of the learners' models of language with the 'correct' model. This may be an overstatement, but there appears to be a lack of exploration or explanation of what learners say about the language they produce: why they produce it or interpret it and what that reveals about their internal models of language.

The field of error analysis might be expected to contribute to understanding learners' models. In fact, of course, Corder is well-known for his contribution to, indeed his creation of the discipline of, error analysis. What is interesting is that although Corder recognises the importance of getting learners to help us to understand what is being intended, the onus of explanation is on the analyst. There is no recognition that it may be possible to get insights from the learner, not just to explain the error, but to give us some understanding of the learner's view of language. Learners may not know why they said what they did but they might be able to comment on what they produced. The gathering of insights from learners themselves into the models of language they hold is in its infancy.

Teachers' and Learners' Models of Language in Action

In considering what we might want to call *lay* views of language, we need to remember that language is all-pervasive, it permeates our thinking, communication, our very being. Hence it is not surprising that language users will have views (however linguistically naive) on the nature of language, of the relation between L1 and L2 learning, the centrality of grammar, the crucial nature of certain phonogical features, the aesthetic nature of certain languages or linguistic features, and so on. Teachers and learners have implicit models of language, which will mediate whatever new models we try to inculcate, which are probably deeply inbuilt, and highly resistant to change. Therefore, at the very least, we need to take such implicit or explicit models into account.

What are these models?

Such models of language can be seen, for example, in what teachers focus on in their teaching and testing, in what and how they plan their lessons, in the feedback they give learners, and the nature of the corrections they offer.

Brumfit, Mitchell & Hooper (1996) report the results of a classroom observation study in which they describe practice in teaching Knowledge about Language (KAL) in English and foreign language classrooms in three secondary schools, together with the results of interviews with teachers and pupils. They argue that the behaviour of teachers and the responses of learners in classrooms are based on their respective models of language.

They show that English teachers' work was text-focused, with explicit talk about the characteristics of particular kinds of texts, both literary and non-literary, and especially at the level of whole texts rather than at the level of sentence structure. Indeed, there was very little evidence of any attention to the teaching of 'language as system', except for one isolated incident of attention to punctuation. The rationale for such teaching seemed to be that 'the establishment of explicit criteria at a fairly high level of generality, e.g. of newspaper writing, would feed through into more effective language performance by their pupils' (1996 :79).

However, in the foreign language classrooms, the area of KAL that received most consistent attention was Language as System, especially grammar and word formation. The dominant rationale 'was the direct contribution [the foreign language teachers] saw it making to the development of pupils' target language proficiency, and this was clearly reflected in the focus of their KAL work on Language as System' (1996: 77).

Pupils' models of language and KAL were explored through group problem-solving tasks, which revealed a competence in both handling language and correcting grammatically deviant sentences, but a very limited ability to comment on and explain language. Although most pupils knew the names of some parts of speech, for example, they were unable to go into much detail or depth, and showed a general lack of sophistication. They also showed very little ability to talk about language learning and how different activities might promote different sorts of learning in any specific way. They attached most importance to their teachers' personal qualities and proficiency in the foreign language.

With respect to language variation, pupils showed a general vague awareness but were unable to be specific about linguistic features that were distinctive for particular genres. Whilst an awareness of their own and others' practices in terms of social and regional variation was evident, 'pupils generally lacked technical vocabulary for discussion of dialectal and social variation and there was considerable confusion and overlap among the concepts employed. Generally their comments seemed to reflect folk-linguistic models current in the community, rather than classroom-derived knowledge' (1996: 84).

Brumfit *et al.* conclude that:

(1) secondary pupils receive largely unrelated messages in KAL from their English and FL teachers;

(2) 'the FL teachers adhered to a fairly traditional view of the usefulness of selected grammatical information', showing little influence of curriculum debates on KAL, and English teachers, whilst seeing introduction to genres and styles as useful, undertook little detailed language analysis;

(3) teachers' own KAL is 'patchy and idiosyncratic';

(4) despite the difference in practice, English and FL teachers both believe there is a direct pay-off for pupils' language development and improved performance as a result of KAL work.

Brumfit *et al.* believe that '[linking [pupils' concerns for low-level accuracy] to understanding of broader discourse issues will significantly help effective language use, in both English and foreign languages' (1996: 85). However, they offer no evidence in support of this belief, and indeed conclude that a long-term research programme is needed to examine the basis for teachers' (and possibly their own) 'beliefs about the positive role of certain kinds of KAL in classroom language development (and for the non-role of others, such as sentence-level work in English)' (1996: 87).

Palfreyman (1993) reports a study of the knowledge about language of four trainee teachers. One pair are native speakers of English, the other non-native speakers. The task of each pair was to plan a lesson for intermediate students on the Present Perfect, and the paper analyses the resulting discussions in terms of the participants' assumptions about language and language learning. Palfreyman identifies two separate approaches to looking at the language system, one of which he labels analytic, 'whereby the informants try above all to establish distinctions, on the basis of context-free principles such as generalised semantic definitions and word-forms. The other ... is a synthetic one, which aims to integrate language in a situational or linguistic context' (p. 222). He suggests that the analytic approach 'could be seen as a native speaker's way of bringing order to his/ her own unconscious linguistic knowledge in the setting of a course of study, while the synthetic approach is a reflection of a competence in English which has developed in an adult NNS, through having to cope in English-speaking situations.' It is interesting to note that different language learning histories might affect the approach to language and to thinking about language: the native speaker trainee teachers seem to assume that their students will 'know' the Present Perfect, in the sense of having met the forms already and that what they need is to have its meaning and use brought to their consciousness, much as they themselves may have learned to reflect on the Present Perfect.

Palfreyman comments on the use of metalanguage in the recorded discussions, reporting negative attitudes to technical terminology (and indeed to 'grammar') on the part of two of the participants (the NNS). He also suggests that the terminology may not necessarily facilitate discussion, but that it is used in power relations to maintain a dominant position in discussions. I have long suspected that this is why teachers use metalanguage in class, to emphasise their position of knowledge and authority, to reinforce their power, and Palfreyman provides some tantalising evidence of this happening (interestingly the person who displays an easy and confident familiarity with and use of metalanguage is male).

What the study shows clearly is that trainee teachers do have models of language that do not necessarily correspond to what is stated in grammar books or indeed in textbooks, and that these may differ systematically for different types of teachers (as Medgyes, 1992, has also suggested: he suggests that NS teachers may have a greater awareness of correct usage whereas awareness of structural patterns may be greater among NNS).

Another interesting study of teachers' metalinguistic awareness is Andrews' pilot study which uses role-played explanations of 'mistakes' to elicit data. Andrews (1996) describes an increased concern in Hong Kong that standards of achievement in English have declined, and an apparently causally related interest in teachers' knowledge about language – their language awareness. His study investigates how teachers explain grammar, by asking both experienced and prospective teachers, native speakers of Chinese attending teacher education courses, to engage in a role play in which they are asked to identify mistakes in an English composition and to 'go over some of the mistakes in class'. The aim was to examine individual teachers' metalinguistic awareness and its interaction with their ability to explain a grammar point. Admittedly the study was exploratory but it clearly reveals teachers not only having difficulty identifying errors, but also showing considerable confusion in their explanations. The feedback they give to students is described as less than helpful, and revealing of the teacher's misunderstanding of rules of English.

However, it would be a mistake to believe that when we find that teachers' knowledge and models are 'imperfect', we must in some way perfect them by a dose of Language Awareness.

An interesting issue to explore is the question Andrews raises at the end of his paper in positing a distinction between declarative versus procedural models of language: i.e. can teachers hold one model, but behave according to another? Is there congruence between beliefs and actions. Do, for example, teachers' rules reflect their beliefs about the nature of language?

In a study of the washback effects of the TOEFL test conducted recently in the USA, Alderson & Hamp-Lyons identified rule-focused teaching as typical of TOEFL classes, as compared with non-TOEFL classes:

> To the extent that the two teachers we observed adjusted their teaching methods when teaching TOEFL classes, we found ourselves questioning their rationale for such change. ... There is no obvious reason why TOEFL classes have to be taught the way they are, and the frequent appearance of teacher-dominated lengthy explanations of grammatical points, with the use of much metalanguage and little opportunity for students to practice or to experiment with what has been said, seems to suggest a rather naive learning theory on the part of the teacher: 'Give students an explanation, they will understand it without problems, and this will automatically change the way they use language and answer test items.' We would like to see much more questioning of what the best way, or more appropriate ways, of teaching TOEFL might be. There ought, in a mature profession, to be much more critical questioning of the assumption that test-taking practice, for example, will automatically lead to improved test performance, or that explanation will lead to internalisation. (1996: 294)

In a recently completed ESRC-funded study of the metalinguistic knowledge of undergraduate students of French in seven British universities (Alderson *et al.*, 1995) we explored the claims made by university teachers of French about their students' knowledge of language. Our results confirmed that levels of knowledge of metalinguistic terminology were surprisingly low, and that the students' ability to state linguistic rules also varied considerably, especially for their native language.

We concluded:

> Any instruction which assumes that students know more than 'noun' or 'verb' will cause problems for many students. (Alderson *et al.*, 1995: 10)

In discussions about the results of this study with the teachers concerned we have suggested that teachers would be well advised to review their use of meta-language, and their assumption that students will learn by exposure. What we do not know, of course, is whether the teachers' models of language are congruent with the students' – indeed we do not even know how well the teachers themselves would fare on our metalinguistic test. I shall discuss below the value of meta-linguistic knowledge in terms of the relationship between a lack of metalinguistic knowledge and proficiency in the foreign language.

What Use is a Model of Language?

I have discussed at some length the importance of taking account of the teachers' and the learners' models of language. I have argued that such models, implicit or explicit, will mediate between any new model we wish them to learn/ acquire/use and their eventual learning and behaviour. I have given some examples of studies attempting to identify these models, and I have suggested that we need more research, both to identify the models, and to begin to explore their relation-ship to behaviour. However, in this final section, I wish to question the use these models might have. As applied linguists we are perhaps bound to believe that having an appropriate model of language will be of benefit, but for what, and how? Interestingly, there have been few attempts to gather evidence to justify such beliefs, as James & Garrett (1991) bemoan.

Nevertheless, it seems reasonable to hypothesise that giving learners linguistic insights might result in an increased ability to use the language. Thus we would expect some degree of relationship between metalinguistic knowledge and lan-guage proficiency. Higher levels of knowledge should be associated with greater accuracy in language use.

Green & Hecht (1992) gave 12 sentences containing common errors in English to 300 German learners of EFL at four broad levels of exposure to English and to 50 comparable English-native-speaker secondary school pupils. The task was to state the rule that had been transgressed in producing the underlined error (cover-ing rules and language that were part of the school curriculum) and to correct the error.

They state the assumptions lying behind the teaching of such rules as follows:

> When teachers teach learners formally the grammar of a foreign language, and when learners ask to be taught it, they are making certain assumptions, even if they do not necessarily make them explicit. The fundamental assump-tion is that it will help the learners to 'get the language right'. Fluency may well, and probably does, come from elsewhere – from some form of practice, no doubt. But if learners are to get beyond the category that Randall Jones

called 'fluent but lousy', it is felt that they will need to formalize the regularities of the language. (1992: 172)

The results showed:

(1) Learners have not learned the rules they have been taught.

(2) Learners can produce correct corrections of the errors.

(3) Native speakers can produce correct corrections but native speakers cannot produce correct rules.

(4) Learners improve in their ability to produce correct corrections as their learning experience increases and their ability to state the transgressed rule correctly also increases, but not so impressively.

(5) 97% of learners can produce the correct correction when they state the transgressed rule correctly: ability to state the rule implies an ability to correct the error.

(6) However, the reverse is not true. 43% of errors corrected were not associated with a correct rule. In 78% of cases where the rule was incorrectly stated, and in 55% of cases where no rule was stated at all, the learners were able to correct the errors.

(7) In the vast majority of cases where native speakers stated the rule incorrectly, and also in cases where no rule was stated, they nevertheless accurately corrected the error.

(8) Some rules were easier to state than others.

(9) The correlation of ability to state the rule correctly with ability to correct the error was significant but only moderate at 0.53.

They conclude:

> The expectation that learners should largely be unable to produce a correct correction if they do not have a correct rule is not only unfounded, the exact reverse is true: learners are still largely able to produce a correct correction when they have an incorrect explicit rule or no explicit rule at all. This suggests that there is no simple relationship between explicit rules and corrections. (Green & Hecht, 1992: 176)

Alderson *et al.* (1995) examined the relationship between metalinguistic knowledge and language proficiency. We found either insignificant or only low correlations between our measures, and decided that metalinguistic ability and linguistic proficiency were relatively unrelated. This was confirmed by factor analyses. We also examined possible changes in the correlation between measures of metalinguistic ability and language proficiency over time. One might have expected that, as students' knowledge of metalanguage gets better, there might be an increase in the relationship between this knowledge and language proficiency. If anything the results show the opposite: when students reach their maximum language proficiency and metalinguistic knowledge (after the Year Abroad, and just before their final examinations) – the correlation between the two drops, instead of increasing.

We therefore concluded that 'there was no evidence to support the belief that students with higher levels of metalinguistic knowledge perform better at French, or that they improve their French proficiency at higher rates than other students. Whilst knowledge about language may be worthwhile in its own right, there is no evidence from this study to justify the teaching of metalinguistic knowledge as a means of improving students' linguistic proficiency' (Alderson et al., 1995: 13).

Conclusion

Language Awareness advocates bringing models of language into classrooms. I have suggested that the evidence for the value of such an approach is scant. Are we witnessing yet another untested fashion, where applied linguists impose their interest in language on unsuspecting and possibly unwilling learners, without regard for their own models, interests and needs?

Applied linguists are fascinated by language. We enjoy noticing special uses of language, changes in pronunciation, grammar, variation by class or region or interlocutor. We are interested in how languages work. We are excited by learning about new approaches to language, be they Universal Grammar and parameter setting, critical discourse analysis, or stylistic approaches to drama. Not surprisingly we convince ourselves that our students should share our enthusiasms or, at the very least, that they need to know something of what we know about language in order to be able to learn or use the language appropriately, properly or, indeed, at all.

Language Awareness is one angle on this. It is not linguistics in another guise, of course, and it is clearly much more than the particular aspects of Knowledge about Language which have been reported in this paper. It encompasses interesting, relevant new approaches to language in its social and individual contexts, the study of language variation over time and by region and class, a growing sensitivity to how people can be manipulated and exploited through language, and an exploration of the power roles that lie behind language use, that determine or shape our social relations.

No doubt some students also find this fascinating. But what effect does this have? How exactly do students benefit from this? What, in short, is the attested value of 'our' models of language, our ways of thinking about language,

language use and language learning, for those who are learning, being taught and being assessed?

My main message is that for teaching and testing, the evidence that we need yet more models is not overwhelming. I have suggested instead that what we need is studies of what implicit and explicit models already exist among teachers and learners, rather than among applied linguists like us. We need to know what such models are like, how they are used, and how they relate to teaching, how they affect behaviour, attitudes, communication, and learning.

References

Alderson, J. C. and Clapham, C. M. (1992) Applied linguistics and language testing: A case study of the ELTS test. *Applied Linguistics* 13 (2), 149–67.

Alderson, J. C., Clapham, C. M. and Steel, D. A. (1995) Metalinguistic knowledge, language aptitude and language proficiency. Final Research Report to ESRC.

Alderson, J. C. and Hamp-Lyons, L. (1996) TOEFL preparation courses: A study of washback. *Language Testing* 13 (3), 280–97.

Alderson, J. C. and Wall, D. M. (1993) Does washback exist? *Applied Linguistics* 14 (2), 115–29.

Andrews, S. (1996) Metalinguistic awareness and teacher explanation. Paper presented at the 3rd International Conference of the Association for Language Awareness, Trinity College Dublin, 4–6 July 1996.

Bachman, L. F. (1990) *Fundamental Considerations in Language Testing*. Oxford: Oxford University Press.

Bonkowski, F. J. B. (1995) Teachers' styles of textbook use in teaching ESL. Unpublished PhD thesis, Lancaster University.

Brumfit, C., Mitchell, R. and Hooper, J. (1996) 'Grammar', 'language' and classroom practice. In M. Hughes (ed.) *Teaching and Learning in Changing Times* (pp. 70–87). Oxford: Blackwell.

Corder, S. Pit (1973) Linguistics and the language teaching syllabus. In J. P. B. Allen and S. Pit Corder (eds) *Readings for Applied Linguistics. The Edinburgh Course in Applied Linguistics*, Vol. 1 (pp. 275–84). London: Oxford University Press.

— (1975) Applied linguistics and language teaching. In *Papers in Applied Linguistics. The Edinburgh Course in Applied Linguistics*, Vol. 2, Chap. 1. London: Oxford University Press.

Esser, U. (1995) Oral language testing. The concept of fluency revisited. Unpublished MA dissertation, Lancaster University.

Fulcher, G. (1993) The construction and validation of rating scales for oral tests in English as a foreign language. Unpublished PhD thesis, Lancaster University.

Fullan, M. G. with Stiegelbauer, S. (1991) *The New Meaning of Educational Change* (2nd edn). London: Cassell.

Green, P. S. and Hecht, K. (1992) Implicit and explicit grammar: An empirical study. *Applied Linguistics* 13 (2), 168–84.

Horak, T. (1996) Multiple perspectives on oral proficiency. Unpublished MA dissertation, Lancaster University.

James, C. and Garrett, P. (eds) (1991) *Language Awareness in the Classroom*. London: Longman.

Katz, J. J. and Fodor, J. A. (1963) The structure of a semantic theory. *Language* 39, 170–210.

McNamara, T. F. (1996) Interaction in second language performance assessment. Plenary address, American Association for Applied Linguistics (AAAL) Annual Conference, Chicago, Ill., 26 March 1996.

Medgyes, P. (1992) A native or a non-native: Who's worth more? *ELT Journal* 46 (4), 340–9.

Munby, J. (1978) *Communicative Syllabus Design*. Cambridge: Cambridge University Press.

Palfreyman, D. (1993) 'Have I got it in my head': Conceptual models of language and learning in native and non-native trainee EFL teachers. *Language Awareness* 2 (4), 209–23.

Trim, J. I. M. (1996) The proposed Common European Framework for the description of language learning, teaching and assessment. Paper presented at the 18th Annual Language Testing Research Colloquium, Tampere, Finland, 31 July to 3 August.

Van Lier, Leo (1992) Not the nine o'clock linguistics class: Investigating contingency grammar. *Journal of Language Awareness* 1 (2), 91–108.

Wall, D. M. (1996) Introducing new tests into traditional systems: insights from general education and from innovation theory. *Language Testing* 14 (3), 334–54.

Wall, D. M. and Alderson, J. C. (1993) Examining washback: The Sri Lankan impact study. *Language Testing* 10 (1), 41–69.

Weir, C. J. (1983) Identifying the language problems of overseas students in tertiary education in the United Kingdom. Unpublished PhD thesis, University of London.

2 A Study of Arabic, Chinese and Malay First and Second Language Punctuation

JONATHAN CHARTERIS-BLACK
The University of Surrey

Abstract

The reaction against prescriptivism has limited interest in punctuation to exclusively diachronic and rhetorical concerns. This study aims to broaden our understanding of punctuation by taking a cross-linguistic perspective. Differences in first language use in Arabic, Chinese and Malay are identified; the second language use of freshmen from Chinese, Malay and Arabic backgrounds is examined, and compared with the English use of freshmen from a British background. The use of the freshmen sample is also compared with that found in published academic writing.

While all groups had difficulty in using intermediate marks as they are used in the sample of published academic writing, a number of language specific differences are identified; these include the frequent omissions of punctuation by both the British and the Arabic groups, and a graphological problem in the use of the comma for which a full stop was often substituted by the Chinese group. The Malay group proved to be the most proficient in punctuation use.

These differences are interpreted with reference to the positive transfer of training in L1 literacy in the case of the Malay group and the influence of negative transfer from the L1 in the case of the Chinese and Arab groups. It appears that the British group are not well trained in punctuation and so they are unlikely to be able to use this skill in academic writing in the L1 let alone in a second language.

It is argued that all freshmen should receive instruction in academic conventions regarding punctuation use if they are to become fully effective in academic writing.

Introduction

Punctuation has not attracted a great deal of attention from linguists or applied linguists; this may either be because it is difficult to prescribe rules for punctuation use – given the range of rhetorical options available to writers – or because difficulties with punctuation are not perceived as likely to impair communication. Whatever the case, it seems that punctuation is either too problematic or not problematic enough to warrant a great deal of interest. Some linguists such as Meyer (1987), Halliday (1989), Nunberg (1990), Nash (1992), Bruthiaux (1993) and (1995) and Dawkins (1995) have shown an interest in the role of punctuation in English, but this has been primarily from either diachronic or rhetorical perspectives. For example, Bruthiaux (1995) explores changes and developments in the system of English punctuation and has identified a declining use in the semi-colon since the 19th century; while Dawkins (1995) claims that rhetorical – as opposed to prescriptive – considerations have an overriding influence on the selection of punctuation marks and illustrates this with reference to literary texts. What both have in common is a concern with variation in punctuation use: a variation which is reflected in the very existence of style manuals which prescribe punctuation conventions for particular groups of writers.

The aims of the present study are to explore variation in punctuation use from a cross-linguistic perspective with reference to the use of punctuation (in English) by freshmen from Arab, Malay, Chinese and British backgrounds. The use of punctuation by these novice writers is compared with that recommended in a style manual and that used in a sample of published academic writing. The differences which emerge may provide some insights into the acquisition of punctuation in both first and second languages. It is hoped that such a study will go some way towards compensating for the lack of importance placed on punctuation in the second language writing instruction literature, as indicated, for example, by its omission from current published sources on writing theory such as Kroll (1990), or Connor (1996).

Background

Initially, it may be helpful to consider the question: is punctuation necessary at all? Some literary styles – such as stream of consciousness – have managed to abandon the system altogether. Clearly, without punctuation, meaning would often be ambiguous, and it is, therefore, an important component of the semantic and syntactic systems giving evidence of where meaningful segments begin and end, and of their relationship to each other. We can see this with reference to some semantic and grammatical functions which are reinforced by punctuation:

Table 1 Semantic functions of punctuation

Colon – Explanatory:

(1) There is one main reason for the decline in the use of punctuation: poor education!

Colon – Contrastive:

(2) Some find punctuation meaningless: others realise its meaning potential!

Colon – Introductory:

(3) Punctuation serves the following purposes: the separation of successive units, the separation of enclosed units, the specification of language function.

Semi-colon – Ellipsis:

(4) Lexical knowledge may be acquired through exposure; grammatical by form focused instruction.

Given its potential to enhance meaning, why, we might ask, is the value of punctuation sometimes questioned? One reason may be the fluidity of the system itself: if semi-colons and dashes are frequently interchangeable, how can we teach which to use? (According to McCaskill (1996) dashes are more emphatic than semi-colons). Punctuation itself can be avoided altogether by substituting a co-ordinate conjunction, for example, 'but' in (2) above, 'and' in (4) above. However, there would be different rhetorical effects concerned with the strength of the semantic relationship between the two related phrases. In (3) the colon has more introductory force than the semi-colon, while the use of a co-ordinate conjunction in (2) or (4) would reduce the semantic and syntactic tension between the two phrases.

In other cases punctuation is more than simply a question of stylistic preference but is an actual semantic and grammatical requirement. For example, some linguistic units, such as non-restrictive clauses, are demarked by punctuation and without it they may no longer be non-restrictive. This can be illustrated with reference to an authentic scenario: baccalaureate examinations are held throughout the French speaking world, but – because of time differences – they cannot be held simultaneously; in 1996 candidates were affected by a typhoon in the New Hebrides and had to resit the examination in May. To describe this situation we can write:

(5) The candidates who had already sat the examination had to resit in May.

(6) The candidates, who had already sat the examination, had to resit in May.

There is an important difference in meaning: In (5) we are restricting the resit to a certain category of candidate (for example, those who had sat the examinations in the New Hebrides) whereas in (6) we are referring to all the candidates who had sat the examination (i.e. including those in France) because the use of commas is obligatory where non-restrictive (or non-dependent) clauses occur in mid-sentence position. The difference is clearly an important one if you took your baccalaureate in 1996!

This semantic function of punctuation also has implications for how a text would sound if it were to be read aloud:

(7) The candidates who had `failed ¬ de`stroyed the examination hall.

(8) The `candidates, ¬ who had failed, ¬ de`stroyed the examination hall.

In (7) we know that some candidates passed and were not involved in the riot, whereas in (8) there is no such restriction, and all the candidates may have failed (which might explain their course of action). The insertion of the commas in (8) increases the number of tone units from two to three by backgrounding the information within them – semantically and phonologically. Punctuation is the written representation of the prosodic features of speech and contributes towards what Nash (1992: 53) describes as 'delivery style'.

Clearly then, punctuation is a rich resource for conveying and enhancing meaning by showing the appropriate relationship between adjacent clauses. At times it is a semantic requirement, at others it is a matter of stylistic preference. Part of its richness lies in that it provides writers with a set of options, thereby frustrating the attempts of style manuals to arrive at a complete and consistent account of punctuation use. It is usually the case that there is a range of possible options available depending on the particular meaning which is intended; it is for this reason that style manuals find it necessary to offer guidelines in punctuation conventions: it is all a question of *whose* conventions. We can see this lack of consensus in the extent to which different punctuation marks are perceived as separating adjacent phrases. While Bruthiaux and Dawkins share the view that there are three degrees of separateness – a top category in which clauses are completely separate, a bottom category in which they are marginally separate and an intermediate category somewhere between these two extremes – they disagree over which marks should be placed in these categories. These differences are summarised in Table 2:

Table 2 Basic functions of punctuation

	Bruthiaux (1995)	Dawkins (1995)
TOP	Full stop	Full stop, semi-colon
INTERMEDIATE/MIDDLE	Semi-colon, colon, dash	Colon, dash
BOTTOM	Comma	Comma, zero mark

Dawes places the semi-colon as indicating as high a degree of separation between clauses as a full stop while Bruthiaux claims it signals less separation. We find little enlightenment when referring to the style manual used in this study – the handbook for technical writers and editors (McCaskill, 1996):

> A colon has the same separating force as a period. It thus brings a sentence almost to a halt.

So now it is unclear whether either the colon or the semi-colon signals the same degree of separation as a full stop.

Dawkins (1995: 538) may be right when he claims writers exploit the rhetorical potential of punctuation by shifting up or down the hierarchy to signal varying degrees of separateness and connection between clauses; he illustrates this with the following example:

(9) John asked for a date when he got the nerve.

(10) John asked for a date, when he got the nerve.

(11) John asked for a date – when he got the nerve.

The shift up the hierarchy from examples (9) to (11) serves to add greater emphasis to the second phrase. However, given the inconsistent treatment of the intermediate marks by these sources, it is little surprise that Dawkins' rhetorical claims for punctuation are based exclusively on literary samples rather than the actual texts of novice writers. In this study there is no assumption that writers have access to such multiple levels and the semi-colon, colon and dash are all grouped together as intermediate marks because of the uncertainty regarding their status. If Bruthiaux (1995) is right in identifying a declining use of the semi-colon since the 19th century we may be shifting from what is basically a three part system to a two part one – with an erosion of the intermediate level. If this is the case (and this study provides further evidence that it is) then the subtle raising and lowering for rhetorical goals – as advised by Dawkins – would no longer be an option since the only choice would be between a comma and a full stop.

It should not be forgotten that in addition to supporting syntax, and enhancing rhetorical and delivery style, punctuation also performs a role in conveying the meaning of utterances by classifying them as questions and exclamations; this may not always be evident from their syntax alone. This diversity of functions is an indication that punctuation is a vital expressive resource of language. In writing education, the use of punctuation can enhance the clarity with which ideas are conveyed, while a lack of such skill may restrict access to the full resources of the written channel. The danger is that language educators' reluctance to make prescriptive statements concerning punctuation may, inadvertently, have undermined their students' ability to employ the system itself.

Punctuation and Second Language Acquisition

In terms of second language acquisition research into the writing of learners from different L1 backgrounds, comparative studies of this type are concerned more with identifying macro-rhetorical features than with identifying the micro-feature of punctuation (Connor & Kaplan, 1987; Dudley-Evans & Swales, 1980; Kaplan, 1966, 1983, 1987; Leki, 1991; Purves, 1988; Swales & Mustafa, 1983). Similarly in second language writing education, the acquisition of the grammar, syntax, lexis, and discourse systems of the target language are usually of more concern to language teachers and learners than the acquisition of the sub-system of punctuation. This view ignores the variation between the way punctuation is used in different languages and overlooks the fact that the acquisition of a finite system – with a very small number of elements – could provide us with insights into the acquisition of other levels, with a greater number of elements, such as morphology and lexis.

The lack of attention given to second language punctuation may be rooted in the assumption that there is a single universal system of punctuation:

> ... Punctuation has been of little interest to linguists concerned with practical problems of developing orthographies to accommodate the phonological systems of hitherto unwritten languages, precisely because the rules of punctuation seem in large measure independent of language-specific features. Thus language planners do not have to devise a new system of punctuation as they do a new orthography: they can simply borrow the system already in place in other writing systems. (Nunberg, 1990: 10)

This is certainly the case with modern standard Arabic:

> In modern times the Arabs have imitated European punctuation, usually – though not always – putting them upside-down. It is now normal to divide prose passages into paragraphs as in Europe. (Haywood & Nahmad, 1965: 13)

Similarly, in Malay, language planners have adopted the western system of punctuation ever since the language was written in Roman as opposed to Arabic script (jawi) in the 15th century (Winstedt, 1927). Modern standard Chinese uses very similar punctuation marks to those in English, although there are some differences – primarily in terms of form as opposed to function; for example, the mark used for a full stop is a small circle rather than a dot. There are also some different conventions of use, for example, angled brackets are used around the title of a book as opposed to quotation marks. There are some additional diacritics in both modern standard Arabic and modern standard Chinese (such as a dot below a Chinese character to indicate emphasis); since the function of these diacritics is primarily phonological in the L1, the L2 learner may be confused by the overlapping syntactic, phonological and semantic roles of punctuation in English.

There are a range of possible factors which may influence the acquisition of L2 punctuation: if there are few major differences in the range and function of punctuation marks between languages, second language punctuation may be no more of a problem for non-native writers than it is for native speaker writers. The same core system can facilitate positive transfer: this would reduce the differences in second language punctuation between these two groups.

Alternatively, in cases where there is not straightforward correspondence between punctuation use in the first and second languages there will be language specific parameters; as Nunberg (1990: 10) points out (my italics):

> It is fair to say, in fact, that there is only one system of punctuation (in the sense, at least, that there is only one Roman alphabet), which is used in all developed Western, alphabetic languages, *subject to the fixing of a few parameters and the establishment of various local conventions and constraints.*

Difficulties with resetting parameters for second language punctuation may lead to negative transfer – especially since the number and nature of the target forms of the second language may lead to cognitive over-loading and an increase in error in those elements of the system which are not perceived as essential to the communication of the writer's meaning. This would be reflected in differences in punctuation use between native and non-native speaker writers.

The research questions for this study are therefore:

(a) What differences are there in the way that groups of learners from different language backgrounds use punctuation?

(b) What types of punctuation errors are made by learners from different language backgrounds?

The answers to these questions should provide us with an indication of the relative importance which should be attached to punctuation in language education.

Methodology

A small corpus of approximately 20,000 words was collected from 100 freshmen enrolling for degree courses at a British university. In addition a sample of 20,000 words was selected from academic articles in the field of applied linguistics. On arrival at the university, all students (including native speakers) are required to take an English language proficiency test to establish their need for language support during their course of study. The test includes two written tasks: a descriptive essay and an expository essay. The freshmen data comprised essays written by 25 students from each of four language backgrounds: Arabic, Chinese, Malay and English. This gave a total of 50 essays for each of the background languages. These particular language backgrounds were selected because it could be anticipated that English punctuation might be problematic, because of script differences between the L1 and the L2, and/or because the first language is not an Indo-European one, thereby reducing the likelihood of positive transfer.

Since language background was selected as the independent variable for this study it was considered acceptable to group together learners from different national backgrounds, but who identified one of the four languages referred to above as both their mother tongue and primary language. The Arabic speaking group (18 males and 7 females) was comprised of learners from Egypt (2), Iraq (3), Kuwait (2), Jordan (4), Lebanon (2), Oman (3), Palestine (1), Saudi (3), Syria (2), Sudan (1), Britain (1) and Yemen (1). The Chinese group (male 10, female 15) and was comprised of students from China (5), Singapore (1), Britain (1) and Taiwan (18). The Malay speaking group (16 males and 9 females) was comprised of learners from Brunei (1), Indonesia (7), Malaysia (14) and Singapore (3). All learners were in the age range 18–23.

The aim of the analysis was to obtain a general profile of punctuation use including target and non-target forms. Initially, the use of three functional categories of punctuation was analysed: the comma, the full stop and the intermediate category of colons, semi-colons and dashes, i.e. those marks whose function lies somewhere between that of the full stop and the comma. No analysis was made of other punctuation features such as brackets, quotation marks, question marks or exclamation marks etc. This was because the corpus was not of a sufficient size to produce reliable data on every element within the sub-system.

The results of the freshman sample were compared with the sample of published academic journals in applied linguistics; these were three articles, one from each of: the *ELT Journal, Applied Linguistics* and *College Composition and Communication.* It was beyond the scope of this study to explore differences in punctuation use in different genres of academic writing. It was necessary to use published texts as a control group because of the possibility of the native speaker freshman group not yet having reached a fully developed stage of punctuation knowledge. It was thought that applied linguists should provide a reliable standard for the conventions of punctuation use in academic writing as language is their domain of research.

Punctuation was classified on the basis of its graphic substance as opposed to its function, for example, in the Chinese data a number of informants used full stops in situations where native speakers would place commas; these were counted as full stops, but they were also, of course, counted as errors as explained below. The rationale for this was to avoid placing an interpretation on the informants' intentions at the graphological level since these could only properly be explored with reference to other data. Subsequently, three categories of punctuation error were identified as follows:

(A) The omission of a punctuation mark in situations where it is necessary (indicated by **0**), for example:

(12) Japan **0** which is the next highest contributor **0** pays nearly 13%. (Arabic mother tongue).

(13) I do not think that just because a country has enough money it should have the final say **0** when other countries **0** with just as valuable opinions **0** can not have its opinion heard as it does not have enough money to pay for this right to an opinion. (English mother tongue).

(B) The insertion of punctuation where none is required (in square brackets), for example:

(14) What I think is[,] nobody is going to be more important than each other. (Mandarin mother tongue).

(15) United Nations reformers should [.] be able to introduce measures that would enable disadvantaged countries to pay in the currency that suits their national interest. (Arabic mother tongue).

(C) The use of the wrong punctuation mark (in square brackets), for example:

(16) I agree with this thought[.] Because when the illness becomes uncurable, it actually makes patients uncomfortable and very ill. (Mandarin mother tongue)

(17) If the person was clever, he would get the degree easier[,] After all, we have to pass some tests to get some qualifications. (Mandarin mother tongue)

The classification of punctuation errors was undertaken by the researcher and a check was undertaken by an experienced University lecturer. Error identification was, at times, problematic because of stylistic variation between the raters even though both were rating from the same source: the internet handbook for technical writers and editors by McCaskill (1996). This source was selected because most students at the University enrol for technical and scientific courses; it advocates an open style in which punctuation is used primarily to prevent misreading. An analysis of inter-rater reliability showed a coefficient of 0.80.

It was important to control the analysis for variations in the length of texts; one would expect the first language group to write more than the second language groups. Therefore, for each punctuation category, the total used, and the number of errors, were divided by the total number of words written by the group and multiplied by 100; this gave a figure for the mean number of punctuation marks and punctuation errors per 100 words of text. This was deemed a suitable unit for comparison as the average length for the total corpus was approximately 100 words per text.

Following the initial identification of errors types, a further analysis was made of the most significant category of error: comma omission. The aim of this third stage in the analysis was to identify the situations in which commas were omitted.

The learner punctuation data was tested using a one-way ANOVA using a multivariate general linear hypothesis testing programme to establish whether there were significant differences in punctuation use between the different groups (Systat, 1989). In situations where significant differences between the groups exceeded those within the groups, a post-hoc comparison using a Scheffe test identified the source of the difference. This made it possible to build up a punctuation proficiency profile for each group of learners and to arrive at a picture of punctuation use according to language background. When second language learners encounter difficulties which are significantly over and above those faced by native speakers we can assume that special attention is required in the second language classroom.

Results
Summary

The analysis clearly showed that there are significant differences regarding accurate and inaccurate punctuation use according to language background, the details of which are described below. However, contrary to expectation, it was the native speaker group which was the least successful in its use of punctuation, at least in terms of accuracy. No group was able to use punctuation as accurately as in the published academic sample and there were language specific difficulties: the English group under-used the comma in circumstances where it would normally be required; the Arabic speaking group under-used the full stop while the Chinese group selected inaccurate punctuation, frequently inserting a full stop where a comma was required. The Malay group encountered the fewest difficulties with punctuation.

Accurate punctuation use

There were significant differences in the overall use of punctuation by learners from different language backgrounds: the Arab and British groups used significantly less punctuation than the Malay and Chinese groups and the academics, while the Malay and Chinese groups used more than the academic sample (although this may be because of different preferences as regards sentence length and sentence construction – see the Discussion section). As regards particular marks, there were significant differences in the use of commas ($p < 0.037$), although the post hoc comparison showed that this was entirely accounted for by difference between the Chinese and the British groups, with the Chinese using significantly more commas. There were also highly significant differences in the use of full stops ($p < 0.001$); the post hoc comparison showed differences between all the groups except the Chinese and the Malay groups, with the Malay group using the most full stops and the Arab group the least.

All groups showed a very low use of intermediate marks, with a significant difference ($p < 0.001$) between the freshman and academic samples; there were no significant differences between the freshman groups. The greater use of intermediate marks in the academic sample suggests that they may be a feature of an academic writing style. The results are summarised in Table 3; two sets of results are given, showing the mean use of each mark per student (irrespective of text length) and the frequency per 100 words of text.

Table 3 English punctuation use

Language background	Commas Mean/ st'dnt	/100 words	Full stops Mean/ st'dnt	/100 words	Intermediate Mean/ st'dnt	/100 words	Total Mean/ st'dnt	/100 words
Arab	7.56	3.84	7.12	3.61	0.16	0.08	14.84	7.53
Malay	9.36	4.08	13.56	5.91	0.36	0.16	23.28	10.15
Chinese	8.36	4.58	10.44	5.71	0.16	0.09	18.96	10.38
British	6.72	2.99	10.36	4.60	0.64	0.28	17.72	7.87
Academic	8.00	4.30	10.37	2.96	0.33	1.23	18.70	8.49

Erroneous punctuation use

As regards the inaccurate use of punctuation, the results for errors were found to be significant at the 0.007 level; that is, the variation between the groups, which exceeds that within the groups, cannot be attributed to chance alone. The post hoc comparison showed that the difference between groups could be accounted for by the large number of punctuation errors made by the British group as compared with the Malay and Chinese groups respectively. The British group made an average of 3.37 errors per 100 words of text, while the Malay group averaged 1.97 and the Chinese group averaged 2.67. In terms of error type, the Chinese group made the most insertions and wrong choices of punctuation – frequently replacing a comma by a full-stop; the Arab group omitted punctuation altogether (especially full stops); the British group also omitted punctuation (especially commas). The British group made approximately twice as many omissions as the Malay and Chinese groups. The results are summarised in Table 4:

Table 4 English punctuation errors

Language background	Omissions Mean/ st'dnt	/100 words	Insertions Mean/ st'dnt	/100 words	Wrong Choice Mean/ st'dnt	/100 words	Total Errors Mean/ st'dnt	/100 words
Arab	4.96	2.52	0.28	0.14	1.16	0.59	6.40	3.25
Malay	3.60	1.57	0.20	0.09	0.72	0.31	4.52	1.97
Chinese	2.32	1.27	0.60	0.33	1.96	1.07	4.88	2.67
British	6.84	3.04	0.12	0.05	0.64	0.28	7.60	3.37
Academic	4.43	2.10	0.30	0.15	1.12	0.56	5.85	2.81

Comma omissions

The most frequent type of omission was omission of a comma; there are two basic functions of the comma: to separate adjacent clauses and, when used in pairs, to enclose a clause, as we have seen in the case of non-restrictive clauses in examples (6) and (8) above. The results for the final stage of the analysis showing different types of comma omission are shown in Table 5:

Table 5 L2 Comma omissions

Language background	Separating Mean	/100 words	Enclosing Mean	/100 words	Total Mean	/100 words
Arab	2.16	1.09	2.28	1.16	4.44	2.25
Malay	1.52	0.66	1.64	0.71	2.23	1.37
Chinese	0.96	0.50	1.00	0.53	1.96	1.03
British	1.96	0.84	3.25	1.39	5.21	2.23
Academic	1.65	0.77	2.04	0.95	3.46	1.72

We can see that the Arab group made the most omissions of the separating comma, and the British group made the most omissions of the enclosing comma.

Overall, the results indicate a number of particular problems for learners from specific language backgrounds, for example, Chinese learners are more likely to select an inaccurate punctuation mark, whereas Arab and British writers are more likely to omit a punctuation mark; this is likely to be an enclosing comma in the case of the British group. Malay learners have fewer problems with punctuation than the other groups. We can conclude that there is a significant difference in the proficiency in English punctuation between learners from different first language backgrounds. However, this is not because of the higher proficiency of the native speaker group in the study; on the contrary, it is because the Malay group made significantly fewer punctuation errors than the Arab or British groups. These findings are illustrated, and their possible causes discussed in the following section.

Discussion and Analysis

Before interpreting specific differences in the use of punctuation between learners from different language backgrounds it is important to consider some general issues influencing our interpretation of the data. First, there is the extent to which differences in punctuation use are the result of a lack of proficiency in punctuation as opposed to differences between other stylistic features of second language writing. For example, the greater use of full stops in the Malay and Chinese texts may simply be the result of shorter sentence length in second language writing. Similarly comma omission by the British group may be related to a preference for longer sentences. Work in contrastive rhetoric has identified a preference for repetition and paraphrase and for a plentiful use of co-ordinate clauses in Arabic writing (Holes, 1983; Sa'adeddin, 1989; Swales & Mustafa, 1983). Future cross-linguistic studies may need to consider the relationship between sentence complexity and the role of punctuation.

If some groups of writers do not attempt non-restrictive clauses as much as others then we would expect to find fewer problems with enclosing commas. Clearly, in measuring punctuation use, we must be aware of the fact that we may simply have identified another dependent variable for measuring underlying rhetorical differences rather than actual proficiency in handling a linguistic sub-system. There is a sense in which we can only be sure that we are gauging underlying proficiency *specifically* in punctuation by considering wrong choices in punctuation rather than simple omissions; however, this would give a restricted account as it would ignore the contribution of punctuation towards writing style.

A further consideration is the extent to which apparent inaccuracies in punctuation are problematic in terms of the writer's ability to communicate ideas in writing. We can see that the main difference between the academic and the freshman data is the much higher use of intermediate marks by the former group. In this sample only 24% of the British group used any intermediate mark, as compared with 28% of the Malay group and 12% of each of the Arab and Chinese groups; only three out of the hundred informants used more than two intermediate punctuation marks in their two essays. These findings provide further evidence of the general decline in intermediate marks identified by Bruthiaux (1995). This is unlikely to be problematic as regards the effective communication of ideas but it is problematic as regards mastery of a target style.

The importance to be placed on the acquisition of punctuation depends on the identification of particular learner needs. Clearly there are discourse communities – such as academics – for whom proficiency in punctuation would be considered a hallmark of their professional status. In this case, native speaker incompetence of the type illustrated in this study can hardly be an argument for disposing of a system which is widely employed in educated published writing. If freshmen are to be viewed as novice academic writers, there is a strong case for including instruction in the use of intermediate marks in academic writing courses for both native and non-native students.

One possible cause of variation in the accuracy with which punctuation is used is the effect of training in domestic education systems; given the wide range of stylistic variation in punctuation use (as already illustrated) it may be that first language educators in some western countries, such as Britain, no longer feel confident in prescribing punctuation use. Given the standardisation of punctuation in the L1s of the non-native groups in this study, and given that the basis for this standardisation is the English system of punctuation, there may well be positive transfer of L1 training; this would account for the better performance of the Malay group as compared with the British group. Another reason could be that teachers in Britain would find some of the uses of punctuation taught in Malaysia too prescriptive; there are likely to be different rates in the evolution of stylistic preferences in different parts of the world. It seems that greater attention to punctuation by educators in western countries, such as Britain, is necessary, if only to facilitate positive transfer of training to second language acquisition. Becoming fully literate in the first language is likely to be beneficial in acquiring second language literacy.

There is also evidence of negative language transfer at work and this can be illustrated with reference to the texts written by Arab freshman. A feature of this data was the omission of the separating as opposed to the delimiting comma and it can be accounted for with reference to the use of a separate lexeme 'wa' to perform this separating function in Arabic:

The chief characteristic of an Arab's written English is his inferior use of subordination and the overuse of co-ordinate constructions. Teachers at the American University of Beirut refer to the *wa wa* method of writing because of the Arabic *wa* 'and', which is exceedingly used as a sentence-connector. (Yorkey, 1974: 14, in Sa'adeddin, 1989: 36)

As separation of co-ordinate clauses is marked lexically there is less need for punctuation: this would help to explain the punctuation omission by the Arab group.

Negative transfer may also be the most likely explanation of some features identified in the Chinese data: full stops are used in place of commas, and there is inconsistency in the use of capitalisation after full stops. The probable reason for this idiosyncratic use of the full stop in English is that since the mark for the full stop in Chinese is a small circle, writers often abbreviate the comma to a dot – when writing in Mandarin – as there is no danger of this being taken as a full stop. We can see evidence of this graphological feature in their L2 writing in the following examples:

(18) It is true that levels of intelligence depend on the age of people[.] and the level of science and technology development. But also[.] it is true[.] that science and technology will develop with time passing.

(19) In the past, the world and the society tended to look down on females[.] many jobs are not suitable for females, but just for males. And now, this circumstance is going to change.

The presence of the intrusive full stop in second language writing can be interpreted as negative transfer at the graphological level. It appears that script related problems in punctuation use were restricted to the Chinese group and did not apply to the Arabic group; we can interpret this as an indication that Arab writers are able to transfer their knowledge of the graphological *content* of punctuation from the L1 (but not necessarily its *function*), whereas this is not always possible for writers whose first language has features which are peripheral to the universal core features of punctuation. While a larger sample based on different genres of writing would be necessary to further substantiate these findings, there is clearly some evidence that learners are transferring the expectations of the first language in second language punctuation use.

If punctuation is a valuable potential resource for enhancing and enriching written communication, then it would seem unwise to deprive learners of the knowledge required to use and exploit this resource to the full. The following examples have been selected from the data to indicate three particular areas where attention is required in both first and second language writing education:

(a) Omission of enclosing marks in non-restrictive and subordinate clauses:

Clearly punctuation omission can lead to a rhetoric which makes greater cognitive demands on the reader. In sentences such (20)–(23) below, commas or dashes should serve the function of backgrounding the elements which are delimited in relation to the rest of the sentence. Their omission makes the sentences more difficult to decode as it is no longer clear which clauses are backgrounded in relation to the others.

(20) It is in a sense very true that to a certain degree, the level of intelligence an individual possesses is fixed. (Arab)

(21) On the other hand, the progress of the scientific researchers and technology in all fields even human sciences shouldn't make us forget or loose hope in the mercy of God who created this technology and is able to create more and more miracles. (Arab)

(22) Poorer countries which pay the minimum amount – $102,000 (in 1993) do not have the same leverage as bigger countries which pay more money which is why some UN reformers want the US to cut down to 10–12%. (British)

(23) Patients who are in the latter stages of the illness should be able with proper guidelines and the backing of the BMA to choose to die at a time of their choosing. (British)

(b) Omission of comma to enclose interrupting elements:

Of less importance to the speed of reader processing are commas which enclose an interrupting element as in (24)–(26) below:

(24) The UN reformers however would like to see this reduced. (British)

(25) The significance to me of the information is not directly obvious. (British)

(26) There are however many things that need to be considered first and a doctor's opinion should be one of the key factors in making the decision. (British)

Inclusion of commas around the interrupting elements ((24) and (26) 'however', (25) 'to me') would provide an indication of the intended delivery style.

(c) Omission of the separating comma:

The omission of the separating comma in (27)–(28) below involves the omission of a single comma as opposed to a pair of commas:

(27) I disagree with this statement because I believe that all people are intelligent but some of them don't know how to upgrade this intelligence and others are lazy they think many times before using their brain. (Arab)

(28) However there are many different opinions on the subject. (British)

The extent to which this is problematic for processing text is probably a function of sentence length: the longer the sentence the greater the need for a separating comma.

Conclusion

We can conclude that all freshmen in this study, in fact, encounter some difficulties with punctuation and that this should be as much a cause for concern to L1 teachers as it is to L2 teachers, as shown, for example, by the failure of all groups to use intermediate marks; however, we have also found that learners from different language backgrounds encounter language specific punctuation difficulties. These can be interpreted with reference to negative transfer at both the rhetorical and graphological levels. These problems should be the concern of all those involved with the provision of language support for university courses and it should not be assumed that freshmen have any degree of familiarity in the conventions of punctuation in academic writing. Such assumptions would be unfounded regarding native and non-native freshmen alike, and, for this reason, all freshmen enrolling in universities should be given instruction in the conventions of punctuation use in the relevant domain.

References

Bruthiaux, P. (1993) Knowing when to stop: Investigating the nature of punctuation. *Language and Communication* 13 (1), 27–43.
— (1995) The rise and fall of the semicolon: English punctuation theory and English teaching practice. *Applied Linguistics* 16 (1), 1–14.
Connor, U. (1996) *Contrastive Rhetoric.* Cambridge: Cambridge University Press.
Connor, U. and Kaplan, R. B. (eds) (1987) *Writing Across Languages: Analysis of L2 text.* Reading, MA: Addison-Wesley.
Dawkins, J. (1995) Teaching punctuation as a rhetorical tool. *College Composition and Communication* 46 (4), 533–48.
Dudley-Evans, T. and Swales, J. (1980) Study modes and students from the Middle East. *ELT Documents 109.* London: The British Council.
Halliday, M. A. K. (1989) *Spoken and Written Language.* Oxford: Oxford University Press.
Haywood and Nahmad (1965) *A New Arabic Grammar.* London: Lund Humphries.
Holes (1983) Textual approximation in the teaching of academic writing to Arab students: A contrastive approach. In J. Swales and H. Mustafa (eds) *The Teaching of ESP in the Arab World* (pp. 228–42). Birmingham, UK: The Language Studies Unit, University of Aston.

40 EVOLVING MODELS OF LANGUAGE

Kaplan, R. B. (1966) Cultural thought patterns in intercultural education. *Language Learning* 16, 1–20.
— (1983) Contrastive rhetoric and second language learning: Notes towards a theory of contrastive rhetoric. *TESOL Quarterly* 17 (4), 609–23.
— (1987) Cultural thought patterns revisited. In U. Connor and R. B. Kaplan (eds) *Writing Across Languages: Analysis of L2 Test* (pp. 9–21). Reading, MA: Addison-Wesley.
Kroll, B. (1990) *Second Language Writing: Research insights for the classroom*. New York: Cambridge University Press.
Leki, I. (1991) Twenty-five years of contrastive rhetoric: Text analysis and writing pedagogies. *TESOL Quarterly* 25 (1), 123–43.
McCaskill, M. K. (1996) *A Handbook for Technical Writers and Editors*. http://sti.larc.nasa.gov/html
Meyer, C. F. (1987) *A Linguistic Study of American Punctuation*. New York: Peter Lang.
Nash, W. (1992) *An Uncommon Tongue: The uses and resources of English*. London: Routledge.
National Language and Lexicology Working Committee and the Press Public and Publication Dept (1990) *The Usage of Punctuation*. The People's Republic of China.
Nunberg, G. (1990) *The Linguistics of Punctuation*. Stanford: CSLI.
Purves, A. C. (1988) *Writing Across Languages and Cultures: Issues in contrastive rhetoric*. Newbury Park, CA: Sage.
Sa'ededdin, M. A. (1989) Text development and Arab–English negative interference. *Applied Linguistics* 10 (1), 36–51.
Swales, J. and Mustafa, H. (eds) (1983) *English for Specific Purposes in the Arab World*. Birmingham, UK: The Language Studies Unit, University of Aston.
Systat (1987) *The System for Statistics*. Evanston, IL: Systat Inc.
Winstedt, R. O. (1927) *Malay Grammar*. Oxford: Clarendon Press.

3 The Epigenesis of Language: Acquisition as a sequence learning problem

NICK ELLIS
University of Wales, Bangor

'Precisely because evolution produced an animal capable of tackling whatever challenge the environment might offer, the answer must be that very few behavioral patterns are rigidly built into the human brain.'
(Leakey & Lewin, 1977: 254)

Constructivist Approaches to Language Acquisition

Human beings are not present in the embryo as miniature complete forms, rather, the development of an embryo consists of the gradual production and organisation of parts. This is the theory of epigenesis: 'the additament of parts budding one out of another' (Harvey, 1653: 272). Human language is no more preformed in the embryo than is human neuroanatomy or human society. This paper advocates a constructivist research agenda which views language acquisition as a problem of *sequence learning* and which denies innate linguistic universals and rules of language as having any causal influence in language acquisition.

Our ability as humans to be impressed by complexity is rarely matched by our talent for scientific understanding. Wonderment makes us posit predeterminism. The theologian William Paley (1828), awed by the intricacy of the human eye and its fittingness for purpose, took its complexity as evidence of God as an artificer who formed it for its purpose. Yet when the focus of study turned towards the development process, it soon became apparent how simple processes of evolution, operating in complex environments, gradually resulted in this impressive phylogenetic feat (Darwin, 1859; Dawkins, 1986). Chomsky (1965), arguably knowing more about the intricacies and universalities of human language than anybody else at the time, took the complexity of these competencies as evidence of an evolutionary process culminating in the provision of linguistic universals represented in a language acquisition device as a general human inheritance. Fifteen years later, he restated this belief as follows: 'We may usefully think of the language faculty, the number faculty, and others, as 'mental organs' [that] develop in specific ways, each in accordance with the genetic program ... multipurpose learning strategies are no more likely to exist than general principles of 'growth of organs' that account for the shape, structure and growth of the kidney' (Chomsky, 1980: 138–9). The Chomskian legacy of Universal Grammar continues to predominate linguistics and second language acquisition.

Yet the last 20 years has seen a revival of approaches to language acquisition, traceable as far back as Locke (1690) and further, that all ideas originate in experience, and that there are no innate ideas. Language is *learned*. These constructivist views of language acquisition, including connectionist approaches (McClelland & Rumelhart, 1986; Levy, Bairaktaris, Bullinaria & Cairns, 1995), functional linguistics (Bates & MacWhinney, 1981; MacWhinney & Bates, 1989), and cognitive linguistics (Lakoff, 1987; Langacker, 1987), believe that Chomsky's (1965) assumption is as suspect as that of Paley. As the study of language turns to consider ontogenetic acquisition processes, it favours a conclusion whereby the complexity of the final result stems from simple learning processes applied, over extended periods of practice in the learner's lifespan, to the rich and complex problem space of language evidence.

Apparent complexity may come more from the problem than from the system which learns to solve it. Simon (1969) illustrated this by describing the path of an ant making its homeward journey on a pebbled beach. The path seems complicated. The ant probes, doubles back, circumnavigates and zigzags. But these actions are not deep and mysterious manifestations of intellectual power. Closer scrutiny reveals that the control decisions are both simple and few in number. An environment-driven problem solver often produces behaviour that is complex only because a complex environment drives it. Language learners have to solve the problem of language. Thus in this case, like that of Simon's ant, it is all too easy to overestimate the degree of control sophistication and innate neurological predisposition required in its solution.

The complexity is in the language, not the learning process:

> Many universal or at least high-probability outcomes are so inevitable given a certain 'problem-space' that extensive genetic underwriting is unnecessary ... Just as the conceptual components of language may derive

from cognitive *content*, so might the computational facts about language stem from nonlinguistic *processing*, that is, from the multitude of competing and converging constraints imposed by perception, production, and memory for linear forms in real time. (Bates, 1984: 188–90, commenting on Bickerton's Language Bioprogram)

Bates refers to Slobin's (1973) operating principles as being good candidates for the learner's processing strategies which result in this extraction of structure. But, constructivist to the core, she elsewhere inquires, where do these strategies come from? They come from the environment, from the cues in language itself (see Bates & MacWhinney, 1981, The Competition Model).

Constructivists are unhappy with nativist explanations simply because they may not be necessary – why posit predeterminism, like magic, when simpler explanations might suffice (Tomasello, 1995; Sampson, 1980)? They are additionally unhappy because the innateness hypothesis has no process explanation – our current theories of brain function, process and development do not readily allow for the inheritance of structures which might serve as principles or parameters of UG. Without such a process explanation, innatist theories are left with a 'and here a miracle occurs' step in their argumentation. Incompleteness of explanation is not a fatal flaw – Mendel was correct long before Crick and Watson provided a process explanation – but we do expect the gaps to be filled eventually, and current neuroscience makes implausible any assumptions about inherited parameter 'switches'.

However, constructivists have an onus beyond criticising other views – they must additionally demonstrate the power of their own explanations. Thus, with the rise of connectionism, much recent constructivist research has concerned computational investigations into what representations can result when simple learning mechanisms for distributional analysis are exposed to complex language evidence. Occam's Razor is influential in their attributions of learning mechanisms: 'Implicit knowledge of language may be stored in connections among simple processing units organized in networks. While the behaviour of such networks may be describable (at least approximately) as conforming to some system of rules, we suggest that an account of the fine structure of the phenomena of language use can best be formulated in models that make reference to the characteristics of the underlying networks' (Rumelhart & McClelland, 1987: 196). Connectionists test such conceptualisations by evaluating the effectiveness of their implementations. Computational practicalities dictate that, for the moment at least, this can only be done in a piecemeal fashion: many separate models now address the acquisition of morphology, phonology, novel word repetition, prosody, semantic structure, and syntactic structure (Levy *et al.*, 1995; MacWhinney, 1987; MacWhinney & Leinbach, 1991; Ellis & Schmidt, in press; Rumelhart & McClelland, 1986). Yet even these simple 'test-tube' demonstrations show that connectionist models can extract the regularities in each of these domains of language and then operate in a rule-like (but not rule-governed) way. The current connectionist enterprise is an effort towards giving these simple learning mechanisms access to the true complexity of the language evidence,

(a) by expanding the models within each domain, improving the low-level representations to provide the learning mechanisms better access to the true richness that is there in the speech stream; and

(b) by combining different sources of evidence (prosodic, semantic, lexical distributional, etc.) to allow interaction between these domains.

We are, as yet, many generations away from even considering putting a connectionist system to the Turing test for native-like language use, but the demonstrations to date are encouragingly persuasive that some of the interesting systematicities of language development that can be described as if they are the product of rule-governed systems, can indeed result from very simple learning mechanisms which statistically abstract the regularities that are present in the evidence of language.

Thus the constructivist view is that language learning results from general processes of human inductive reasoning being applied to the specific problem of language. There is no language acquisition device specifiable in terms of linguistic universals, principles and parameters, or language-specific learning mechanisms. Rather, language is cut of the same cloth as other cognitive *processes*, but it is special in terms of its cognitive *content*. Learners' language comes not directly from their genes, but rather from the structure of adult language, from the structure of their cognitive and social cognitive skills, and from the constraints on communication inherent in expressing non-linear cognition into the *linear* channel provided by the human vocal-auditory apparatus (Bates, Thal & Marchman, 1991).

This leads us to the characterisation of language as a *sequence* learning problem.

(L)anguage, as a complex, hierarchical, behavioral structure with a lengthy course of development ... is rich in sequential dependencies: syllables and formulaic phrases before phonemes and features ..., holophrases before words, words before simple sentences, simple sentences before lexical categories, lexical categories before complex sentences, and so on. (Studdert-Kennedy, 1991: 10)

This assumption that each of the subsystems, phonology and syntax, evolved hierarchically by repeated cycles of differentiation and integration, promises an understanding of language development in functional terms. 'It is a general rule of both phylogeny and ontogeny that complex structures evolve by differentiation of smaller structures from larger. Accordingly, we do not expect children to build words from phonemes, as adults do; rather, we should expect phonemes to emerge from words' (Studdert-Kennedy, 1991: 16). Studdert-Kennedy goes on to point out that 'similar principles must apply to the development of word classes and syntactic structures, a fact not generally recognized in developmental psycholinguistics.' Nor is it sufficiently recognised in the study of second- or foreign-language acquisition.

The remainder of this paper will concentrate on the sequence learning aspects of the acquisition of language. It will argue that (i) individual learners' verbal short-term memory ability is a good predictor of their language learning aptitude, (ii) much of fluent language use is memory based, following the idiom principle rather than open-class models, (iii) simple sequence analysis of large collections of language allows the automatic induction of grammatical word-class, and (iv) analysis of learners' speech, both in L1 and L2, demonstrates how statistical learning processes of chunking and sequence analysis characterise their progression to fluency. I have gathered evidence for some of these claims before (Ellis, 1996). Rather than repeat this here, I will try in the main to bolster the arguments with additional material.

Language Learning as Sequence Analysis

One possible description of language learning is as follows. *Language learning is the learning and analysis of sequences:*

(a) the learner must acquire sound sequences in words,

(b) the learner must acquire word sequences in phrases, and

(c) these sequences form the database for the abstraction of grammar.

(a) Learning word structure involves identifying the categorical units of speech perception, their particular sequences in particular words, and their general sequential probabilities in the language. (b) Learning discourse structure largely involves learning particular sequences of words in stock phrases and collocations. The idiom principle underlies much of fluent language use and language learners need to acquire particular sequences of words in particular phrases, and the general sequential probabilities of words in the language. (c) Learning the grammatical word-class of a particular word, and learning grammatical structures more generally, involves in large part the automatic implicit analysis of the word's sequential position relative to other words in the learner's stock of known phrases which contain it.

This is not an explanation, it is a description which, while hardly contentious, clearly demonstrates how sequence analysis pervades all levels of language processing.

Verbal sequencing ability predicts language aptitude

One advantage of this focus on sequence analysis is that it allows insight into individual differences in language aptitude. Individuals differ in their ability to repeat phonological sequences (this is known as phonological short-term memory [STM] span). This ability to repeat verbal sequences (for example, new phone numbers or nonwords like 'sloppendash') immediately after hearing them, is a good predictor of learner's facility to acquire vocabulary and syntax in first, second, and foreign language learning. Ellis (1996) reviews a wide range of evidence for this: (i) phonological STM span predicts vocabulary acquisition in L1 and L2, (ii) interfering with phonological STM by means of articulatory suppression disrupts vocabulary learning, (iii) repetition and productive rehearsal of novel words promotes their long-term consolidation and retention, (iv) phonological STM predicts syntax acquisition in L1 and L2, (v) phonological rehearsal of L2 utterances results in superior performance in receptive skills in terms of learning to comprehend and translate L2 words and phrases, explicit metalinguistic knowledge of the detailed content of grammatical regularities, acquisition of the L2 forms of words and phrases, accuracy in L2 pronunciation, and grammatical fluency and accuracy (Ellis & Sinclair, 1996).

So what is the involvement of phonological memory in language learning? Ellis (1996) presents an account which is based on the basic learning mechanism of 'chunking'. This term was coined by George Miller in his classic review of short-term memory (Miller, 1956). It is the development of permanent sets of associative connections in long-term storage and is the process which underlies the attainment of automaticity and fluency in language.

> A chunk is a unit of memory organization, formed by bringing together a set of already formed chunks in memory and welding them together into a larger unit. Chunking implies the ability to build up such structures recursively, thus leading to a hierarchical organization of memory. Chunking appears to be a ubiquitous feature of human memory. Conceivably, it could form the basis for an equally ubiquitous law of practice. (Newell, 1990: 7)

Chunking allows us to bootstrap our way into language: Repetition of sequences in phonological STM allows their consolidation in phonological long-term memory (LTM). Perception of frequent sequences, and the more frequent subsequences within them, allows their chunking in phonological LTM. The same cognitive system which stores long-term memories of phonological sequences perceives input of phonological sequences. Thus the tuning of phonological LTM to regular sequences allows more ready perception of input which contains regular sequences. Regular sequences are thus perceived as chunks and, as a result, L2-experienced individuals' phonological STM for regular sequences is greater than for irregular ones. To give examples in the orthographic domain, you perceive the sequences '123456789' and 'orthographic domain' much more readily than their scrambled counterparts '831742965' and 'gdmnirhrtocohoipaa' and are concomitantly more likely to be able to successfully repeat them shortly afterwards. Such influences of LTM on STM make the relationship between these systems truly reciprocal and underlie the development of automaticity (LaBerge & Samuels, 1974; McLaughlin, 1987). This is an epigenetic view of *language* whereby acquisition is the additament of *chunks* budding one out of another.

Experience of our environment leads to modification of our schemata, our schemata direct our exploration of the environment, our exploration samples the available information in the environment, and thus the cycle continues. The same systems which perceive language represent language. Thus the 'cycle of perception' (Neisser, 1976) is also the 'cycle of learning' – bottom-up and top-down processes are in constant interaction.

Chunking and the idiom principle

It is easy to see this cycle of learning in vocabulary acquisition: As learners' L2 vocabulary extends, as they practise hearing and producing L2 words, so they automatically and implicitly acquire knowledge of the statistical frequencies and sequential probabilities of the phonotactics of the L2. Their input and output modules for L2 processing begin to abstract knowledge of L2 regularities, thus to become more proficient at short-term repetition of novel L2 words. And so L2 vocabulary learning lifts itself up by its bootstraps. But the same processes operate at all levels of language. Language reception and production are mediated by learner's representations of chunks of language: 'Suppose that, instead of shaping discourse according to rules, one really pulls old language from memory (particularly old language, with all its words in and everything,) and then reshapes it to the current context: "context shaping", as Bateson puts it, "is just another term for grammar"' (Becker, 1983: 218). This is why elicited imitation tests serve so well as measures of second-language competence (Lado, 1965; Bley-Vroman & Chaudron, 1994).

As we analyse language performance, so the underlying chunks become readily apparent. Sinclair (1991), as a result of his experience directing the Cobuild project, the largest lexicographic analysis of the English language to date, proposed *the principle of idiom* –

a language user has available to him or her a large number of semi-preconstructed phrases that constitute single choices, even though they might appear to be analysable into segments. To some extent this may reflect the recurrence of similar situations in human affairs; it may illustrate a natural tendency to economy of effort; or it may be motivated in part by the exigencies of real-time conversation. However it arises, it has been relegated to an inferior position in most current linguistics, because it does not fit the open-choice model. (Sinclair, 1991: 110)

Rather than its being a rather minor feature, compared with grammar, Sinclair suggests that for normal texts, the first mode of analysis to be applied is the idiom principle, since most of text is interpretable by this principle. Comparisons of written and spoken corpora demonstrate that collocations are even more frequent in spoken language than they are in the written Cobuild corpus (Butler, 1995). Collocations and stock phrases are viewed with just the same importance in FL research where they are known as holophrases (Corder, 1973), prefabricated routines and patterns (Hakuta, 1974), formulaic speech (Wong-Fillmore, 1976), memorised sentences and lexicalised stems (Pawley & Syder, 1983), lexical phrases (Nattinger & DeCarrico, 1992), or formulas (R. Ellis, 1994). An important index of native-like competence is that the learner uses idioms fluently. So language learning involves learning sequences of words (frequent collocations, phrases, and idioms) as well as sequences within words.

With the benefit of hindsight, it comes as no surprise that language is acquired in this way. The formation of chunks, as stable intermediate structures, is the mechanism underlying the evolution and organisation of many complex hierarchical systems in biology, society, and physics (Simon, 1962; Dawkins, 1976).

Working out how words work – The distributional analysis of memorised collocations

As we analyse word sequence chunks, so we discover that they have characteristic structures all of their own. Linguists call these regularities grammar. And if we take a bottom-up approach, and simply describe the distributional properties of words in chunks, so we discover that something very close to traditional grammatical word-class information emerges. Kiss (1973) provided the first computational model of the acquisition of grammatical word class from accumulating evidence of word distributions. An associative learning program was exposed to an input corpus of 15,000 words gathered from tape recordings of seven Scottish middle class mothers talking to their children who were between one and three years of age. The program read the corpus and established associative links between the words and their contexts (here defined as their *immediate successor*). Thus, for example, the program counted that *the* was followed by *house* 4.1% of the time, by *horse* 3.4%, by *same* 1%, by *put* never, etc., that *a* was connected to *horse* 4.2%, to *house* 2.9%, to *put* never, etc., etc. For computational reasons (this work was done in the days of punched cards) such 'right-context' distributional vectors were only computed for 31 frequent words of the corpus. These vectors constituted a level of associative representation which was a network of transitions. Next a classification learning program analysed this information to produce connections between word representations which had strengths determined by the degree of similarity between the words in terms of the degree to which they tended to occur together after a common predecessor (i.e. the degree of similarity based on their 'left-contexts'). This information formed a level of representation which was a network of word similarities. Finally the classification program analysed this similarity information to produce a third network which clustered them into groups of similar words. The clusters that arose were as follows: (*hen sheep pig farmer cow house horse*) (*can are do think see*) (*little big nice*) (*this he that it*) (*a the*) (*you I*). It seemed that these processes discovered word classes which were nounlike, verblike, adjectivelike, articlelike, pronounlike, etc. Thus the third level of representation, which arises from simple analysis of word distributional properties, can be said to be that of word-class. Kiss argues that in this way language learners can bootstrap their way into discovering word classes. More recent, and much larger, demonstrations show that such bootstrapping results from a variety of analysis methods including statistical, recurrent neural network, or self-organising map models (Sampson, 1987; Charniak, 1993; Finch & Chater, 1994; Honkela, Pulkki & Kohonen, 1995).

The Cobuild project represents the largest descriptive enterprise of this type for English, and three key conclusions of this research are (i) that is impossible to describe syntax and lexis independently, (ii) that syntax and semantics are inextricable, and (iii) that language is best described as being collocational streams where patterns flow into each other (often going over the clause boundary).

> Through the reliability and objectivity of the computer evidence, verbs can be divided according to the pattern, and pattern can be seen to correlate with meaning – that is to say, verbs with similar patterns have similar meanings ... We can now see that this relation between meaning and pattern is inevitable – that meaning and usage have a profound and systematic effect on one another. (Sinclair, forward to Collins Cobuild Grammar, 1996: iv)

Thus the Collins Cobuild (1996) analysis of English verbs shows that there are perhaps 100 major patterns of English verbs (of the type, for example, V *by* amount: the verb is followed by a prepositional phrase which consists of the preposition *by* and a noun group indicating an amount as in 'Their incomes have dropped by 30 per cent', 'The Reds were leading by two runs', etc.). Verbs with the same Comp pattern share meanings (the above-illustrated pattern is used by three meaning groups: (i) the 'increase' and 'decrease' group [inc. 'climb', 'decline', 'decrease', 'depreciate', etc.], (ii) the 'win' and 'lose' group [inc. 'lead', 'lose', and 'win'], (iii) the' overrun' group [inc. 'overrun', 'overspend']). Any Comp pattern is describable *only* in terms of its lexis.

Perhaps surprisingly, Chomsky's recent accounts of syntax in the Minimalist Program for Linguistic Theory (MPLT) (Chomsky, 1992, 1995) share this emphasis on lexis and sequence analysis. (Chomsky, 1989, emphasis added) stated: 'there is only one human language apart from the lexicon, and *language acquisition is in essence a matter of determining lexical idiosyncrasies.*' Within the MPLT,

> *differences between languages are attributed to differences between the features of lexical items in the languages* and specifically between the features of lexical items belonging to the functional categories AGR and Tense ... Vs and Ns are taken from the lexicon fully inflected with inflectional affixes ... specific bundles of these features of the category AGR and T are lexical items and *differences between the sets of bundles available in the lexicon account for cross-linguistic syntactic differences between languages.* (Marantz, 1995: 366, emphasis added)

Thus this corpus linguistic approach and the MPLT are alike in focusing on lexis as being at the centre of syntax. In both accounts, syntax acquisition reduces to vocabulary acquisition – the analysis of how words work in sequence. As Singleton (1996) quipped, this is the linguistic analogue of the economic maxim: 'Look after the pennies and the pounds will look after themselves'.

Sequences in learner talk

We have seen that as powerful computers are used for the distributional analysis of large language corpora, so they demonstrate the underlying chunks of language and the ways in which lexical items, with their particular valences and subcategorisation requirements, operate in these patterns. The final part of the argument for viewing language learning as sequence learning is a demonstration from analyses of collections of *learners'* language that they acquire collocations in their path to fluency, and that their analyses of these chunks gives them the information about lexical idiosyncrasies that allows later more open-class productions. This evidence is there for both L1 and L2.

L1

Tomasello (1992), from whom I have taken the notion of language epigenesis, begins his book, *First Verbs: A Case Study of Early Grammatical Development*, with the following observation from Wittgenstein: '

Language games are the forms of language with which a child begins to make use of words ... When we look at the simple forms of language the mental mist which seems to enshroud our ordinary use of language disappears. We see activities, reactions, which are clear-cut and transparent. On the other hand we recognise in these simple processes forms of language not separated by a break from our more complicated ones. We see that we can build up the more complicated forms from the primitive ones by gradually adding new forms. (Wittgenstein, *The Blue Book:* 1969: 17)

Tomasello (1992) kept a detailed diary of his daughter Travis' language between one and two years old. On the basis of a fine-grained analysis of this corpus he proposed the Verb Island hypothesis: Young children's early verbs and relational terms are individual islands of organisation in an otherwise unorganised grammatical system. In the early stages the child learns about arguments and syntactic marking on a verb-by-verb basis, and ordering patterns and morphological markers learned for one verb do not immediately generalise to other verbs. The reason for this is that the nascent language learners do not have any adult-like syntactic categories or rules, nor do they have any kind of word class of verb that would support generalisations across verbs.

Particular summary observations supporting this claim were as follows:

There is individuality and contextedness everywhere, signs of broad-based rules nowhere. T did bring order and systematicity to her language during her 2nd year of life, but it was a gradual, constructive process. It did not resemble in any way the instantaneous and irrevocable setting of para-meters ...

T's earliest three-or-more-word sentences (18–21 months) were almost all structured by verbs. The vast majority of these involved straight-forward co-ordinations of already produced word combinations (93%), preserving in almost all cases the established ordering patterns of the constituents (99%).

T began marking the syntagmatic relations in these three-or-more-word sentences through the use of contrastive word order and prepositions. She did this, however, on a verb-by-verb basis. By far the best predictor of the arguments and argument markings that T used with a particular verb at a particular time was previous usage of that verb, not same time usage of other verbs.   (Tomasello, 1992: 264–6)

He states his conclusion for epigenesis as follows:

It is not until the child has produced or comprehended a number of sentences with a particular verb that she can construct a syntagmatic category of "cutter", for example. Not until she has done this with a number of verbs can she construct the more general syntagmatic category of agent or actor. Not until the child has constructed a number of sentences in which various words serve as various types of arguments for various predicates can she construct word classes such as noun or verb. Not until the child has constructed sentences with these more general categories can certain types of complex sentences be produced. (Tomasello, 1992: 273–4)

Other analyses of child language corpora point to similar conclusions. For example, Lieven, Pine & Dresner Barnes (1992) show formulae to be both frequent (children's first 100 words typically contain about 20 formulae) and productive (in providing templates which, following analysis, are converted into lexically based patterns).

L2

No observation is entirely theory-free. Yet we are fortunate to have some descriptions of stages of L2 proficiency which were drawn up in as atheoretical way as possible by the American Council on the Teaching of Foreign Languages (ACTFL) (Higgs, 1984). The ACTFL (1986) Oral Proficiency Guidelines include the following descriptions of novice and intermediate levels:

Novice Low:
Oral production consists of *isolated words and perhaps a few high-frequency phrases.* Essentially no functional communicative ability.

Novice Mid:
Oral production continues to consist of *isolated words and learned phrases* within very predictable areas of need, although quantity is increased. Vocabulary is sufficient only for handling simple, elementary needs and expressing basic courtesies. Utterances rarely consist of more than two or three words and show frequent long pauses and repetition of interlocutor's words.

Novice High:
Able to satisfy partially the requirements of basic communicative exchanges *by relying heavily on learned utterances but occasionally expanding these through simple recombinations of their elements.* Can ask questions or make statements *involving learned material.* Shows signs of spontaneity, although this falls short of real autonomy of expression. *Speech continues to consist of learned utterances* rather than of personalized, situationally adapted ones. Vocabulary centres on areas such as basic objects, places, and most common kinship terms. *Pronunciation may still be strongly influenced by first language.*

Intermediate:
The intermediate level is characterized by an ability to create with the language *by combining and recombining learned elements,* though primarily

in a reactive mode; initiate, minimally sustain, and close in a simple way basic communicative tasks; and ask and answer questions.

Intermediate Low:
Able to handle successfully a limited number of interactive, task-oriented social situations. Can ask and answer questions, initiate and respond to simple statements, and maintain face-to-face conversation, *although in a highly restricted manner* and with much linguistic inaccuracy. Within these limitations, can perform such tasks as introducing self, ordering a meal, asking directions, and making purchases. Vocabulary is adequate to express only the most elementary needs. *Strong interference from native language may occur.*

Intermediate-Mid:
Able to handle successfully a variety of uncomplicated, basic communicative tasks and social situations. Can talk simply about self and family members. Can ask and answer questions and participate in simple conversations on topics beyond the most immediate needs, e.g. personal history and leisure-time activities. *Utterance length increases slightly, but speech may continue to be characterized by frequent long pauses, since the smooth incorporation of even basic conversational strategies is often hindered as the speaker struggles to create appropriate language forms. Pronunciation may continue to be strongly influenced by first language* and fluency may still be strained.

(ACTFL, 1986, emphases added)

It is clear that L2A, like L1A, is characterised by the acquisition of collocations and chunks of language which are slowly analysed on a word-by-word basis to allow the determination of grammatical word class and c-selection. L2A additionally demonstrates significant transfer from L1, as is predicted by constructivist accounts which emphasise sequential analysis (Ellis, 1996) or the competition of multiple cues (MacWhinney, in press).

Conclusions

Fluent language users have had tens of thousands of hours on task. They have processed many millions of utterances involving tens of thousands of types presented as innumerable tokens. The evidence of language has ground on their perceptuo-motor and cognitive apparatus to result in complex competencies which can be described by formal theories of linguistics such as UG. It is more than a 'simplifying assumption' that language learning 'can be conceptualized as an instantaneous process' (Chomsky, 1976: 14–15). It is an error which compounds into the fallacy of predeterminism.

Language is like the majority of complex systems which exist in nature and which empirically exhibit hierarchical structure (Simon, 1962). And like these other systems, its complexity emerges from simple developmental processes being exposed to a massive and complex environment. We are enlightened when we substitute a process description for a state description – when we describe development rather than the final state.

Meteorology has its rules and principles of the phenomena of the atmosphere which allow the prediction of weather. Geology has its rules and principles to describe and summarise the successive changes in the earth's crust. But these 'rules' are the descriptions and heuristics of science. They play no causal role in shifting even a grain of sand or a molecule of water. It is the interaction of water and rocks which smoothes the irregularities and grinds the pebbles and sand. UG is like the other -ologies with its principles and parameters to describe language, and the rules of UG have a similar causal status.[1] The proper study of language acquisition is to chart the course by which perceptual, motoric, and cognitive functions induce structure, from undifferentiated novice performance to that remarkably differentiated native-like competence. There is a more relevant Universal which concerns process and learning rather than content: it is to be found in efforts to rationalise intelligence in terms of models of optimal (Bayesian – see Chater, 1995; Gigerenzer & Murray, 1987) inference in the presence of uncertainty. Language acquisition researchers would do well to mirror language learners in investigating the conditional probabilities of words in sequence.

Note

1. This should not be taken to deny any role of pedagogical rules in language learning. Unlike rocks or clouds, humans are reactive to verbal instruction. Thus some parts of their environment can be made more salient (e.g. by 'grammatical consciousness raising' or 'input enhancement' or 'focus on form'), and learners are more likely to learn about the *parts of the environment* to which they selectively *attend* (Ellis, 1994, 1995).

References

ACTFL (1986) *The ACTFL Proficiency Guidelines.* Yonkers, NY: The American Council on the Teaching of Foreign Languages.

Bates, E. (1984) Bioprograms and the innateness hypothesis. *Behavioral and Brain Sciences* 7, 188–90.

Bates, E. and MacWhinney, B. (1981) Second language acquisition from a functionalist perspective. In H. Winitz (ed.) *Native Language and Foreign Language Acquisition, Annals of the New York Academy of Sciences* 379, 190–214.

Bates, E., Thal, D. and Marchman, V. (1991) Symbols and syntax: A Darwinian approach to language development. In N. A. Krasnegor, D. M. Rumbaugh, R. L. Schiefelbusch, and M. Studdert-Kennedy (eds) *Biological and Behavioral Determinants of Language Development* (pp. 29–66). Hillsdale, NJ: Lawrence Erlbaum Associates.

Becker, A. L. (1983) Toward a post-structuralist view of language learning: A short essay. *Language Learning* 33, 217–20.

Bley-Vroman, R. and Chaudron, C. (1994) Elicited imitation as a measure of second-language competence. In E. Tarone, S. M. Gass and A. D. Cohen (eds) *Research Methodology in Second-Language Acquisition* (pp. 245–61). Hillsdale, NJ: L. Erlbaum.

Butler, C. (1995) Between lexis and grammar: Repeated word sequences and collocational frameworks in Spanish. Paper presented to the 5th Dyffryn Conference on Vocabulary and Lexis, Cardiff, 31 March – 2 April.

Charniak, E. (1993) *Statistical Language Learning*. Cambridge, MA: MIT Press.

Chater, N. (1995) Neural networks: The new statistical models of mind. In J. P. Levy, D. Bairaktaris, J. A. Bullinaria, and P. Cairns (eds) *Connectionist Models of Memory and Language* (pp. 207–27). London: UCL Press.

Chomsky, N. (1965) *Aspects of a Theory of Syntax*. Cambridge, MA: MIT Press.

— (1976) *Reflections on Language*. London: Temple Smith.

— (1980) *Rules and Representations*. NY: Columbia University Press.

— (1989) Some notes on economy of derivation and representation. *MIT Working Papers in Linguistics* 10, 43–74.

— (1992) A minimalist program for linguistic theory. *MIT Occasional Papers in Linguistics, 1* (published (1993). In K. Hale and S. J. Keyser (eds) *The View from Building 20: Essays in linguistics in honor of Sylvian Bromberger* (pp. 1–52). Cambridge, MA: MIT Press.

— (1995) Bare phrase structure. In G. Webelhuth (ed.) *Government and Binding Theory and the Minimalist Program* (pp. 383–420). Oxford: Blackwell.

Collins Cobuild (1996) *Grammar Patterns 1: Verbs*. London: Harper Collins.

Corder, S. P. (1973) *Introducing Applied Linguistics*. Harmondsworth: Penguin.

Darwin, C. (1859) The origin of the species. Reprinted. London: Penguin.

Dawkins, R. (1976) Hierarchical organisation: A candidate principle for ethology. In P. P. G. Bateson and R. A. Hinde (eds) *Growing Points in Ethology* (pp. 7–54). Cambridge: Cambridge University Press.

— (1986) *The Blind Watchmaker*. Harlow: Longman.

Ellis, N. C. (1994) Implicit and explicit processes in language acquisition: An introduction. In N. Ellis (ed.) *Implicit and Explicit Learning of Languages* (pp. 1–32). London: Academic Press.

— (1995) Consciousness in second language acquisition: A review of field studies and laboratory experiments. *Language Awareness* 4, 123–46.

— (1996) Sequencing in SLA: Phonological memory, chunking, and points of order. *Studies in Second Language Acquisition* 18, 91–126.

Ellis, N. C. and Schmidt, R. (in press, 1997). Morphology and longer-distance dependencies: Laboratory research illuminating the A in SLA. *Studies in Second Language Acquisition* 19: 2.

Ellis, N. C. and Sinclair, S. (1996) Working memory in the acquisition of vocabulary and syntax: Putting language in good order. *Quarterly Journal of Experimental Psychology* 49A, 234–50.

Ellis, R. (1994) *The Study of Second Language Acquisition*. Oxford: Oxford University Press.

Finch, S. and Chater, N. (1994) Learning syntactic categories: A statistical approach. In M. Oaksford and G. D. A. Brown (eds) *Neurodynamics and Psychology* (pp. 295–321). London: Academic.

Gigerenzer, G. and Murray, D. J. (1987) *Cognition as Intuitive Statistics*. Hillsdale, NJ: Lawrence Erlbaum.

Hakuta, K. (1974) Prefabricated patterns and the emergence of structure in second language acquisition. *Language Learning* 24, 287–98.

Harvey, W. (1653) *Anatomical Exercises.* Translated by Richard Lowdnes, London.

Higgs, T. V. (1984) (ed.) *Teaching for Proficiency, the Organising Principle.* Lincolnwood, IL: National Textbook Company.

Honkela, T., Pulkki, V. and Kohonen, T. (1995) Contextual relations of words in Grimm Tales, analysed by self-organising maps. In F. Fogelman-Soulie and P. Gallinari (eds) *Proceedings of International Conference on Artificial Neural Networks: ICANN-95* (pp. 3–7). EC2 et Cie, Paris.

Kiss, G. R. (1973) Grammatical word classes: A learning process and its simulation. In G. H. Bower (ed.) *The Psychology of Learning and Motivation: Advances in research and theory* Vol. 7 (pp. 1–41). New York: Academic Press.

LaBerge, D. and Samuels, S. J. (1974) Towards a theory of automatic information processing in reading. *Cognitive Psychology* 6, 292–323.

Lado, R. (1965) Memory span as a factor in second language learning. *IRAL, III* 123–9.

Lakoff, G. (1987) *Women, Fire, and Dangerous Things: What categories reveal about the mind.* Chicago: University of Chicago Press.

Langacker, R. (1987) *Foundations of Cognitive Grammar.* Stanford, CA: Stanford University Press.

Leakey, R. E. and Lewin, R. (1977) *Origins: What new discoveries reveal about the emergence of our species and its possible future.* London: Futura.

Levy, J. P., Bairaktaris, D., Bullinaria, J. A. and Cairns, P. (eds) (1995) *Connectionist Models of Memory and Language.* London: UCL Press.

Lieven, E. V. M., Pine, J. M. and Dresner Barnes, H. (1992) Individual differences in early vocabulary development: Redefining the referential-expressive dimension. *Journal of Child Language* 19, 287–310.

Locke, J. (1690) *An Essay Concerning Human Understanding.* Edition of P. H. Nidditch, Oxford, 1975.

McClelland, J. L and Rumelhart, D. E. (eds) (1986) *Parallel Distributed Processing: Explorations in the microstructure of cognition, Vol. 2: Psychological and biological models.* Cambridge, MA: MIT Press.

McLaughlin, B (1987) *Theories of Second Language Acquisition.* London: Edward Arnold.

MacWhinney, B. (ed.) (1987) *Mechanisms of Language Acquisition.* Hillsdale, NJ: Erlbaum.

— (in press) Second language acquisition and the competition model. In A. M. B. de Groot and J. F. Kroll (eds) *Tutorials in Bilingualism: Psycholinguistic perspectives.* Hillsdale, NJ: Lawrence Erlbaum.

MacWhinney, B. and Bates, E. (1989) (eds) *The Crosslinguistic Study of Sentence Processing.* New York: Cambridge University Press.

MacWhinney, B. and Leinbach, J. (1991) Implementations are not conceptualisations: Revising the verb learning model. *Cognition* 40, 121–57.

Marantz, A. (1995) The minimalist program. In G. Webelhuth (ed.) *Government and Binding Theory and the Minimalist Program* (pp. 349–82). Oxford: Blackwell.

Miller, G. A. (1956) The magical number seven, plus or minus two: Some limits on our capacity for processing information. *Psychological Review* 63, 81–97.

Nattinger, J. R. and DeCarrico, J. S. (1992) *Lexical Phrases and Language Teaching.* Oxford: Oxford University Press.

Neisser, U. (1976) *Cognition and Reality: Principles and implications of cognitive psychology.* San Francisco: Freeman.

Newell, A. (1990) *Unified Theories of Cognition.* Cambridge, MA: Harvard University Press.

Paley, W. (1828) *Natural Theology* 2nd edn. Oxford: J. Vincent.
Pawley, A. and Syder, F.H. (1983) Two puzzles for linguistic theory: Native-like selection and native-like fluency. In J. C. Richards and R. W. Schmidt (eds)*Language and Communication* (pp. 191–225). London: Longman.
Rumelhart, D. E. and McClelland, J. L. (1986) On learning the past tense of English verbs. In J. L. McClelland, D. E. Rumelhart and the PDP Research Group (eds) *Parallel Distributed Processing: Explorations in the microstructure of cognition, Vol. 2: Psychological and biological models* (pp. 216–71). Cambridge, MA: MIT Press.
— (1987) Learning the past tense of English verbs: Implicit rules or parallel distributed processes? In B. MacWhinney (ed.) *Mechanisms of Language Acquisition* (pp. 195–248). Hillsdale, NJ: Erlbaum.
Sampson, G. R. (1980) *Making Sense.* Oxford: Oxford University Press.
— (1987) Probabilistic models of analysis. In R. Garside, G. Leech and G. Sampson (eds) *The Computational Analysis of English* (pp. 16–29). Harlow, Essex: Longman.
Simon, H. A. (1962) The architecture of complexity. *Proceedings of the American Philosophical Society* 106, 467–82. Reprinted in H. A. Simon (1969) *The Sciences of the Artificial.* Cambridge, MA: MIT Press.
— (1969) *The Sciences of the Artificial.* Cambridge, MA: MIT Press.
Sinclair, J. (1991) *Corpus, Concordance, Collocation.* Oxford: Oxford University Press.
Singleton, D. (1996) Overview of the lexical processing symposium. Paper presented at the 11th World Congress of Applied Linguistics, Jyväskylä, Finland, 4–9 August, 1996.
Slobin, D. I. (1973) Cognitive prerequisites for the development of grammar. In C. A. Ferguson and D. I. Slobin (eds) *Studies of Child Language Development* (pp. 175–208). New York: Holt Rinehart Winston.
Studdert-Kennedy, M. (1991) Language development from an evolutionary perspective. In N. A. Krasnegor, D. M. Rumbaugh, R. L. Schiefelbusch and M. Studdert-Kennedy (eds) *Biological and Behavioral Determinants of Language Development* (pp. 5–28). Hillsdale, NJ: Lawrence Erlbaum Associates.
Tomasello, M. (1992) *First verbs: A case study of early grammatical development.* Cambridge: Cambridge University Press.
— (1995) Language is not an instinct. *Cognitive Development* 10, 131–56.
Wittgenstein, L. (1969) *Preliminary Studies for the Philosophical Investigations generally known as the Blue and Brown Books by Ludwig Wittgenstein.* Oxford: Blackwell.
Wong-Fillmore, L. (1976) The second time around. Unpublished doctoral dissertation, Stanford University.

4 A New Measure of Lexical Diversity[1]

DAVID MALVERN and BRIAN RICHARDS
The University of Reading

Abstract

Language researchers frequently use indices of lexical diversity as develop-mental measures in studies of, for example, first and second language acquisition, deafness, Down's syndrome and language impairment, linguistic input to chil-dren, in clinical practice with the language delayed, and in forensic linguistics.

The most common approach has been to divide the number of Types by the number of Tokens to produce the *Type–Token Ratio* (TTR). The TTR, and the measures derived from it (Root-TTR, Log-TTR, for example), are flawed, how-ever, being dependent on the size of the sample of Tokens used. Other procedures such as Mean Segmental TTR neither fully exploit the data nor provide a universal base for comparison.

Here, the problems with standard measures and the ways in which their use can lead to anomalous results are demonstrated. Mathematical models of the relationship between TTR and Token size are shown to be a basis for producing a valid measure of lexical diversity which is independent of sample size and can be made more readily accessible to researchers and clinicians than previous mathe-matical approaches.

Introduction

Language researchers frequently use indices which reflect the range of vocabulary in a text or conversation. Such measures are variously referred to either positively as indices of 'lexical diversity', 'lexical range', 'vocabulary richness', 'flexibility', 'verbal creativity' (Fradis *et al.*, 1992), and 'lexical range

58

and balance' (Crystal, 1982), or, particularly in the field of language disorder, negatively as an index of 'repetitiveness' (Perkins, 1994). Although lexical diversity is sometimes treated as indicating vocabulary size, and has indeed been used to estimate total vocabulary size in children (Wagner *et al.,* 1987), it is usually regarded as assessing language in use.

Measures of lexical diversity have been applied in many areas of linguistic investigation. These include stylistics, forensic linguistics, studies of emotional disorders, schizophrenia, stress and anxiety, and the speeches of politicians. While our approach to measuring lexical diversity is relevant to these and other areas, our starting point is the spoken and written language of those developing both first and second languages. This includes the study of language delay and language impairment. From an extensive review of the literature (Richards & Malvern, submitted for publication, 1997) we have found that many researchers working in these contexts, and particularly in L1 research, are not fully aware of some of the pitfalls of assessing diversity of vocabulary.

The Type–Token Ratio

If we conceptualise lexical diversity as the number of different words in a stretch of discourse, it is clear that the longer the discourse, the greater the number of different words (types) there will be. For any given text, the relationship between the number of word tokens sampled and the number of word types is curvilinear, a relationship which researchers have been trying to model mathematically at least since the work of Thompson & Thompson in 1915.

A common measure, which many have erroneously believed to be independent of sample size is the Type–Token Ratio (TTR). This is simply the number of different words divided by the total number of words. TTR has a maximum value of 1.0, reflecting total diversity (all the words are different), and will tend towards zero as repetitiveness increases.

The Problem with TTR

It is often supposed that because a proportion has been calculated, TTR is independent of sample size. In studies of child language in particular, TTR is recurrently assumed to be constant; for example, Miller (1981) states:

> The consistency of this measure makes it enormously valuable as a clinical tool. For example, if a normal hearing child's TTR is significantly below 0.50 we can be reasonably certain the sparseness of vocabulary is *not* an artefact of SES but is probably indicative of a language-specific deficiency. (Miller, 1981: 41)

Miller derived this figure from tables supplied in Templin's seminal work *Certain Language Skills in Children* (Templin, 1957). Templin provides undoubtedly reliable data of numbers of tokens and types found in an analysis of 50 utterances from groups of 60 children at eight different ages. Templin comments on an apparent consistency:

> By comparing Tables 60 [number of different words] and 61 [total number of words used], the proportion of different words used to all words uttered in 50 remarks is apparent. This ratio is approximately one different word for slightly over every two words uttered. This ratio shows little variation over the range tested and among subsamples, sex and SES groups. (Templin, 1957: 115)

Simple calculations on Templin's figures do produce average TTRs for the different ages all between 0.434 and 0.469 (see Table 1). This proved to be a powerful source for the later assumption of constancy.

Table 1 TTRs calculated for Templin's data for 50 utterances

Age of Sample	Mean Tokens	Mean Types	TTR on Means
3	204.9	92.5	0.451
3.5	232.9	104.8	0.450
4	268.8	120.4	0.448
4.5	270.7	127.0	0.469
5	286.2	132.4	0.463
6	328.0	147.0	0.448
7	363.1	157.7	0.434
8	378.8	166.5	0.440

Adapted from Templin (1957): Tables 60 and 61, p. 116

Nonetheless, TTR is not a constant, but decreases with increasing size of token sample. The reason is straightforward – as the number of Tokens increases, the available pool of new Types diminishes and the more Tokens in any sample, the greater the probability of repetitions. In theory, a large enough sample would exhaust the speaker's (or writer's) repertoire of word Types, and thereafter the ratio would tend to zero.

The relationship between TTR and sample size has been demonstrated for the transcript of one two-year-old by Richards (1987). From this it can be seen that for the same child, Sian, a TTR either above or below 0.5 can be obtained depending on how large a segment of transcript is chosen for the type and token counts (see Figure 1). That the 0.5 threshold is spurious is also evident from the fact that our analysis of Prince Charles' 1989 speech about the state of the English language obtains a TTR of only 0.36 (834 Types from 2,350 Tokens), and the TTR of 'Macbeth' is 0.20 (Chen & Leimkuhler, 1989).

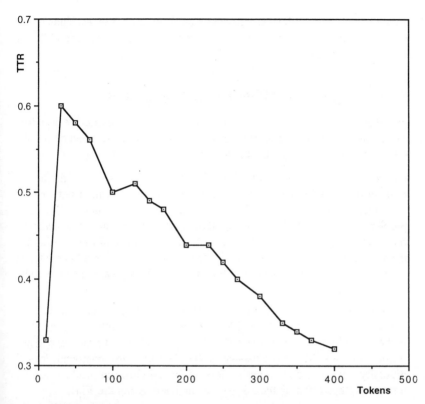

Figure 1 TTR vs Tokens reported by Richards for Sian

Researchers have been aware of the relationship between TTR and sample size since the 1940s (e.g. Johnson, 1944), and more recent publications in the field of child language (e.g. Hess *et al.*, 1986, 1989; Richards, 1987) have drawn attention to the problem. Nevertheless, that this problem is not widely appreciated has given rise to flawed methodology and numerous anomalous results in the child language literature where TTRs based on varying numbers of tokens have been used for comparisons within or between subjects. What is needed is a methodology which overcomes the difficulty and is capable of explaining Templin's otherwise authoritative results.

Two typical examples of anomalies in well-known research in child language are Bates *et al.* (1988) where for children at 28 months TTRs were negatively correlated with Mean Length of Utterance and another vocabulary measure, and Lieven's case study of two children (1978) whose TTRs fell as children got older and their MLU increased. Such results, though counter-intuitive for something which is meant to be a developmental measure, are possible because as children advance they both speak more and use longer utterances. Thus when calculating TTRs, the larger numbers of words from more advanced children tend too overwhelm their gains in lexical diversity.

Variations of TTR and Other Diversity Measures

Several measures try to reduce variation in sample size, or attempt transformations intended to remove the effect of sample size. These are listed below. As we will show, however, they are all unsatisfactory.

(1) One recent approach in a study of clinical assessments has been to divide the number of types by the number of utterances (Yoder *et al.*, 1994). However, this measure is confounded by two factors. Firstly, there is the same problem as with TTR: the more utterances in the denominator, the lower the ratio. Secondly, subjects with longer utterances will tend to score higher because each additional utterance will then be more likely to add new types to the numerator. Unlike TTR, it is possible for values greater than one to be obtained if the number of types exceeds the number of utterances.

(2) A more common approach is to standardise the number of utterances from which TTRs are calculated (e.g. Fletcher, 1985 used 100 utterances) and this is the one adopted by the SALT (Systematic Analysis of Language Transcripts) software (Miller & Chapman, 1993). However, this confounds lexical diversity with utterance length: more advanced children produce longer utterances, thus inflating the token count and depressing the TTR.

(3) Some researchers summarise the length of recording and calculate, for example, TTR for 50 minutes (Broen, 1972), or number of types in 10 minutes. The latter has recently been advocated by Catherine Snow and colleagues (e.g. Snow, 1996). The problem here is that lexical diversity and volubility are confounded: children receive higher scores simply because they talk more. Note that the former solution (calculating TTR) has the opposite effect: high volubility *depresses* TTRs.

(4) A possible solution is to use a sample which is so large that the effects of variations in sample size are negligible. Richards (1987) suggested that the curve which plotted TTR against the number of tokens flattened out after 400–500 tokens. In practice, however, samples of this size are the exception in child language research, especially when dealing with atypical populations. Besides, Wachal & Spreen (1973) have shown with aphasic patients that even with samples of over 1,000 words, variations in the token count compromise the validity of the measure.

(5) Another solution is to calculate all TTRs from a standard number of tokens (e.g. Hess *et al.*, 1989). The disadvantage here is that the number chosen is

the equivalent of the smallest sample, thus wasting data from larger samples and reducing reliability.

(6) It has been claimed that a number of *transformations* of TTR produce values which are independent of the number of tokens. These include Types divided by the square root of the number of Tokens; Types divided by the square root of *twice* the number of Tokens; and the logarithm of the number of Types divided by the logarithm of the number of Tokens. These alternative measures are related to TTR as follows:

TTR   = Types/Tokens: the Type–Token Ratio;

CTTR   = Types/√(2 Tokens): Carroll's lexical diversity measure
                              (Corrected TTR);

RTTR   = Types/√Tokens: Guiraud's 'indice de richesse' (Root TTR);

LogTTR = logTypes/logTokens: Herdan's index (Bilogarithmic TTR).

In spite of the advantages claimed for these transformations, for example, Broeder *et al.*'s preference for Guiraud's index (Broeder *et al.,* 1993), all have been shown to be affected by sample size, whether in the speech of preschool (Hess *et al.,* 1986; Richards, 1987), or school-aged children: (Hess *et al.,* 1989), the writing of L2 English students (Arnaud, 1984), or literary texts (Ménard, 1983). With regard to their reliability Hess *et al.,* (1986) found none of the four measures above to show any advantage over the others and all to require the same sample sizes to be reliable. For TTR, CTTR and RTTR this should come as no surprise, given their mathematical connectedness:

Where V = the number of types and N = the number of tokens,

if   TTR = V/N,

then CTTR = V/√(2N) = TTR x √(N/2),

and RTTR = V/√N = CTTR x √2 = TTR x √N.

Provided these measures are calculated from exactly the same set of Types and Tokens, and allowing for rounding errors, the only difference between them is the scaling of the independent variable (N) (not of the dependent variable (V)). Two conclusions follow from this. Firstly, any apparent reduction of the relationship with sample size is an artefact of the change in scale and will be accompanied by a reduction in the sensitivity of the measure owing to the use of smaller units. Secondly, the measures will be perfectly correlated with each other and their reliability will be identical.

(7) Several measures of lexical diversity, mainly referred to in literary studies and stylistics, are based on rank frequencies (the number of words which

occur once in a sample, the number occurring twice, and so on). These include Yule's Characteristic K, Michéa's Constant, and Yule-Herdan's V_m. To our knowledge, only Yule's Characteristic K has been used in the study of child language (Hess et al., 1986). These indices have been rejected as either sensitive to sample size or uninterpretable (Hess et al., 1986; Ménard, 1983).

(8) One measure which has not gained currency in the child language field is the Mean Segmental TTR (e.g. Wachal & Spreen, 1973) – the average TTR for successive segments of text containing a standard number of tokens. This has the advantage over (5) above that it makes more use of the data available, but even here, the size of segment will be determined by the size of the smallest sample, and segments based on small samples will fail to be sensitive to repetition of words over larger stretches of discourse.[2]

(9) In a study of the relationship between the speech environment and children's auxiliary verb development, Richards (1990) computed correlations between the frequency of yes–no questions addressed to children and the subsequent growth in the diversity of auxiliary verb types in each sample. Initially, Richards attempted to control for variations in sample size by calculating the range of auxiliary forms per verb phrase. However, as might be expected from the discussion above, there was a negative correlation between this measure and the number of verb phrases produced. The solution adopted was to use the number of auxiliary verb types as the dependent variable and remove the influence of variation in the number of verb phrases by regression analysis. Nevertheless, while this solution may be preferable to a total lack of control for sample size, it has the disadvantage of applying a linear regression model to a relationship which is far from being linear.

We have shown above that commonly used methods of reducing the effects of variations in sample size, whether by standardising time of recording or number of utterances, by using mathematical transformations or rank frequency measures, are all problematic. Mean Segmental TTR seems to be the most successful approach to date (see point 8, above), but is still subject to reservations. MSTTRs are only comparable if they have been calculated from equal sized segments. In other words, a child's MSTTR100 cannot be validly compared with the same or another child's MSTTR500. Just as TTR falls with increasing sample size, so MSTTRs will be smaller for larger segments.

A New Measure of Lexical Diversity

The important point which has been missed by all these methods is that when TTR is plotted against token size (N) it falls from a maximum value of one for an utterance of one token (hence one type) in a curve which for a very large token size will eventually tend towards zero (when all known types have already been used, and further utterances can only depress the value of TTR). It is this curve as a whole which is characteristic of the individual rather than any particular value of TTR on it.

Modelling lexical diversity mathematically is an exercise in probability and various mathematical studies have been carried out. Although most have concentrated on different aspects of vocabulary use, there are two studies which have modelled types or a form of TTR against N directly. Brainerd (1982) chose to model Types(V) as a function of Tokens (N) in the form $V = N^{\frac{\ln M}{\ln N}}$, and showed that: Log-TTR $= A - B \ln N^{\frac{\ln M}{\ln N}}$ where M is the theoretical total productive vocabulary of the subject. He then went on to plot graphs of these functions for, and calculate the parameters A and B (which characterise the lexical diversity or repetitiveness) from, empirical (adult) data. Sichel (1986), however, produced the most complete model to date by making appropriate approximations to arrive at:

$$V = \frac{2}{bc}\left[1 - e^{\left(-b\left(\{1 + cN\}^{\frac{1}{2}} - 1\right)\right)}\right].$$

Neither of these models is mathematically simple and both need *two* parameters to describe any individual's lexical diversity. What is required is a simplification which depends on only *one* parameter and is robust enough to provide a measure of sufficient accuracy for the relatively small samples found in child language and other research.

We have explored Sichel's model graphically and algebraically, and have shown both that it does account for the behaviour of TTR, CTTR, etc. and that empirical values for his two parameters (b,c) can be found for samples of child language data. We have also demonstrated that while both parameters are small, c is the more significant at small N while b determines the longer range behaviour for large N (Malvern, 1991). Consequently, an approximation to Sichel's equation for low token samples can be used to yield the model

$$TTR = \frac{2}{DN}\left[(1 + DN)^{\frac{1}{2}} - 1\right]$$

with only one parameter, D, which can be derived empirically for sample utterances. It is this model, and any subsequent simplifications of it, which we are proposing as a solution to the problem of providing a reliable and comparable measure of lexical diversity.

The method we propose is to calculate points on the TTR versus Types curve for individuals by averaging sub-samples of progressively larger token size from transcript data. By adjusting D to find the best fit between the resulting empirical curve and curves predicted by the model, the value of D for the subject can be evaluated to use as a base for an index of lexical diversity which makes full use of all the data in a transcript or other form of language sample. As D is a parameter of the whole curve it is not like TTR and derivatives (including Mean Segmental-TTR) which are calculated for only one particular value on it. It is not, therefore, dependent on the size of the token sample used.

As an illustration, the transcript for Sian used by Richards (1987) to show empirically that TTR is a decreasing function of Tokens has been recalculated using the averaging method described above and the results are plotted together with the best fitting curve calculated from the model in Figure 2.

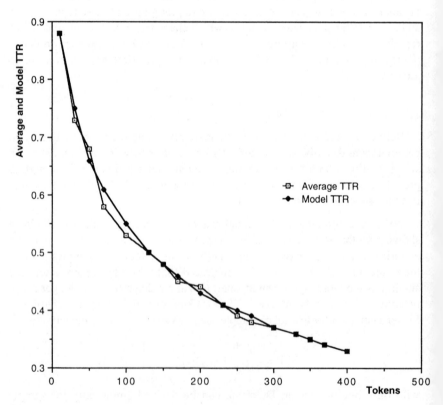

Figure 2 Average and model values for Sian's TTR

Moreover, it can be shown that this model is compatible with Templin's data without making the assumption that TTR remains constant for growing children. Larger and more diversely deployed vocabularies result in TTR against Token curves which are less steep than smaller vocabularies with greater repetition. Consequently, the curve for an individual showing greater vocabulary diversity will lie above that for a child displaying less. If the common sense assumption is made that as children grow their vocabulary increases and they make more use of it, they would be expected to move onto progressively higher and higher lying curves.

As Table 1 shows, the TTRs calculated for older children from Templin's data are on average for larger Token sizes. For them, then, the points used are further along their TTR against Token curves and achieving the same value of TTR for larger Token size shows that they are on a higher TTR against Token curve. Figure 3 shows how progressively less steep TTR against Token curves can be drawn to pass through the points calculated from Templin's data.

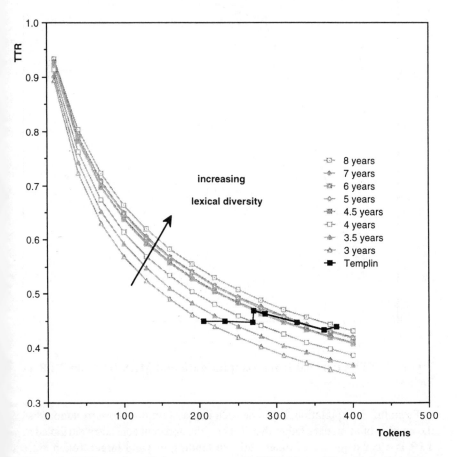

Figure 3 TTR against Token curves to fit TTRs from Templin's data for given ages

The best form of an index based on D is still under investigation, but for illustrative purposes, one method which produces an appropriate scaling for comparison with TTR and referred to here as Malvern-Richards-Sichel D* (MRS D*) is a simple linear transformation MRS D* = 1-10D. Figure 4 shows the values of MRS D* calculated on the values of D derived from the curves drawn in Figure 3. Unlike the TTRs which are more or less constant for Templin's data, MRS D* changes with age.

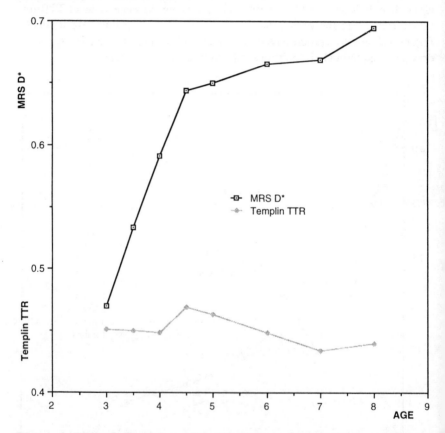

Figure 4 TTRs derived from Templin data and MRS D* from TTR vs Token curves in Figure 3

From this interpretation, it can be seen that as Templin chose to standardise the number of utterances rather than Tokens, the apparent constancy attributed to TTR is a consequence of older children tending to yield larger Token sizes simply because on average they produce longer utterances. Calculating TTRs for older children on the larger Token sizes of their longer utterances under-represents the deployment of their anticipated larger vocabularies compared to the TTRs from the shorter utterances of younger samples. This kind of analysis is also likely to explain the many studies in the literature which report a lack of correlations of TTR with other language development measures.

Conclusions and Further Implications

We have illustrated the drawbacks of conventional approaches to measuring lexical diversity and outlined a new solution. Currently we are attempting to make this solution more widely available by developing software which will operate on a language sample transcribed in a standard format, such as CHAT format from the CHILDES project (MacWhinney & Snow, 1990). The software will automate the process of calculating and averaging TTRs for subsamples of given token sizes, and produce a series of such averages for subsamples of increasing token size. A curve-fitting procedure and subsequent transformation of the value obtained for D will provide an index which can be used by other researchers and practitioners.

It should be noted that the problems associated with TTR and, potentially, their solution, are relevant to any measure which attempts to quantify a range of linguistic behaviours. Most obviously, this applies to measures such as TTRs calculated for different word classes – a TTR for nouns and a TTR for verbs will not be comparable unless the number of noun tokens is the same as the number of verb tokens. In addition, the linguistic literature contains a number of examples of type/type ratios. In the investigation of the use of rare words, for example, a proportional measure which compares the number of rare word types with the total number of word types will be a negative function of the total number of types (Sichel, 1986). Similarly, several recent investigations have calculated the proportion of types which belong to certain word classes. This includes Bates *et al.*'s (1988) style measures. For example, 'referential style' is calculated as 'the proportion of the child's vocabulary consisting of common nouns' (p. 97), that is to say the number of different nouns divided by the number of different words sampled. The relationship of such measures with sample size will vary according to the *relative* size of each closed set and the distribution of each set of items in language samples.

Notes

1. The publication of this paper has been supported by the Economic and Social Research Council (Grant no. R0000 22 1995) as part of the project 'A new research tool: mathematical modelling in the measurement of lexical diversity'.
2. We would like to thank Brian MacWhinney for making this point.

References

Arnaud, P. J. L. (1984) The lexical richness of L2 written productions and the validity of vocabulary tests. In T. Culhane, C. Klein Bradley and D. K. Stevenson (eds) *Practice and Problems in Language Testing: Papers from the International Symposium on Language Testing* (pp. 14–28). Colchester: University of Essex.

Bates, E., Bretherton, I. and Snyder, L. (1988) *From First Words to Grammar: Individual differences and dissociable mechanisms.* Cambridge: Cambridge University Press.

Brainerd, B. (1982) The Type–Token relation in the works of S. Kierkegaard. In R. W. Bailey (ed.) *Computing in the Humanities.* North-Holland Publishing.

Broeder, P., Extra, G. and van Hout, R. (1993) Richness and variety in the developing lexicon. In C. Perduc (ed.) *Adult Language Acquisition: Cross-linguistic perspectives* Vol. I: Field Methods (pp. 145–232). Cambridge: Cambridge University Press.

Broen, P. (1972) The verbal environment of the language-learning child. *ASHA Monograph 17.*

Chen, Y. S. and Leimkuhler, F. F. (1989) A type–token identity in the Simon-Yule model of text. *Journal of the American Society for Information Science* 40, 45–53.

Crystal, D. (1982) *Profiling Linguistic Disability.* London: Edward Arnold.

Fletcher, P. (1985) *A Child's Learning of English.* Oxford: Blackwell.

Fradis, A., Mihailescu, L. and Jipescu, I. (1992) The distribution of major grammatical classes in the vocabulary of Romanian aphasic patients. *Aphasiology* 6, 477–89.

Hess, C. W., Haug, H. T. and Landry, R. G. (1989) The reliability of type–token ratios for the oral language of school age children. *Journal of Speech and Hearing Research* 32, 536–40.

Hess, C. W., Sefton, K. M. and Landry, R. G. (1986) Sample size and type–token ratios for oral language of preschool children. *Journal of Speech and Hearing Research* 29, 129–34.

Johnson, W. (1944) Studies in language behavior: I. A program of research. *Psychological Monographs* 56, 1–15.

Lieven, E. V. M. (1978) Conversations between mothers and young children: Individual differences and their possible implication for the study of child language learning. In N. Waterson and C. E. Snow (eds) *The Development of Communication* (pp. 173–87). Chichester: Wiley.

MacWhinney, B. and Snow, C. E. (1990) The child language data exchange system: An update. *Journal of Child Language* 17, 457–72.

Malvern, D. D. (1991) Interpreting the type–token ratio: A mathematical model. Poster displayed at the 1991 Child Language Seminar, University of Manchester.

Ménard, N. (1983) *Mesure de la Richesse Lexicale.* Geneva: Slatkine.

Miller, J. F. (1981) *Assessing Language Production: Experimental Procedures.* London: Arnold.

Miller, J. F. and Chapman, R. (1993) *SALT: Systematic Analysis of Language Transcripts, Version 3.0.* Baltimore: University Park Press.

Perkins, M. (1994) Repetitiveness in language disorders: A new analytical procedure. *Clinical Linguistics and Phonetics* 8, 321–36.

Richards, B. J. (1987) Type/token ratios: What do they really tell us? *Journal of Child Language* 14, 201–9.

— (1990) Predictors of auxiliary and copula verb growth. Paper presented at the Fifth International Congress for the Study of Child Language, Budapest, Hungary.

Richards, B. J. and Malvern, D. D. (submitted for publication, 1997) Quantifying lexical diversity in the study of language development. Reading: The University of Reading, New Bulmershe Papers.

Sichel, H. S. (1986) Word frequency distributions and type–token characteristics. *Mathematical Scientist* 11, 45–72.

Snow, C. E. (1996) Change in child language and child linguists. In H. Coleman and L. Cameron (eds) *Change and Language* (pp. 75–88). Clevedon: BAAL in association with Multilingual Matters.

Templin, M. C. (1957) *Certain Language Skills in Children.* Minneapolis: The University of Minnesota Press.

Thompson, G. H. and Thompson, J. R. (1915) Outlines of a method for the quantitative analysis of writing vocabularies. *British Journal of Psychology* 8, 52–69.

Wachal, R. S. and Spreen, O. (1973) Some measures of lexical diversity in aphasic and normal language performance. *Language and Speech* 16, 169–81.

Wagner, J. R., Altmann, G. and Köhler, R. (1987) Zum Gesamtwortschatz der Kinder. In K. R. Wagner (ed.) *Wortschatz-Erwerb* (pp. 128–42). Bern: Peter Lang.

Yoder, P. J., Davies, B. and Bishop, K. (1994) Adult interaction style effects on the language sampling and transcription process with children who have developmental disabilities. *American Journal on Mental Retardation* 99, 270–82.

5 Applying a Lexical Profiling System to Technical English

JAMES MILTON and TOM HALES
University of Wales, Swansea

Introduction

This paper addresses some of the problems inherent in answering the question of 'how technical' a given sample of text is. Primarily, we wish to evaluate the efficacy of a profiling method which quantifies and summarises the degree of 'difficulty' of a text, as a function of the word frequency profile. In order to do this we have used an already existing lexical profiling system, that used by Meara (1993), Laufer & Nation (1995) and Meara *et al.* (1997).

Although considerable work has been done to pin down the nature of what is generally referred to as 'Technical English' (for example, see Farrell, 1990), there is still much discussion about what actually constitutes technical language, whether English or otherwise. Technical language need not in theory be difficult language. But it is a commonplace in the consideration of technical language to acknowledge the presence of a technical register which includes terms and expressions not used in general English. Such terminology is frequently seen as deliberately excluding non-specialists and as intentionally incomprehensible to them (see, for example, Yule, 1985: 245). It may be that a feature of technical language is that it includes infrequent vocabulary, although this connection has not to our knowledge been explicitly demonstrated. This paper addresses this shortcoming directly.

What is of interest is the extent to which a measurement of the 'difficulty' of a text relates to a general definition of 'Technical English', i.e. whether it captures the *nature* of technical vocabulary. The approach we adopt here uses a model of lexical profiling based on word frequency using the categorisations devised by

Nation (1986). The output may be seen as both providing a measure of text difficulty and, in that, identifying at least some of the characteristic features of 'Technical English', thereby contributing something to our understanding of the relationship between technical language on the one hand and difficult language on the other.

Intuitive Impressions and Reality

Foreign Language teachers make decisions on degrees of technicality or difficulty every day by intuition. But, as many corpus linguists have emphasised, intuition can be rather hit-and-miss (for example, Sinclair, 1991). Authors repeatedly comment on the fact that the content of nearly all language course-books is based on linguistic intuitions of what is required, and this has not always compared well with research into what happens linguistically in the real world (see Willis, 1990). Therefore, something more scientific than intuition is required.

The lexical profiles we have produced are similar to those of Meara (1993) in that we are attempting to measure the demands made by the vocabulary of a text on the learners who must decode it. Meara admits that there are problems, not least of oversimplification, in this technique. For example, the method lemmatises text prior to analysis but there are no allowances made for poly-semous words or words with unusual derivations. However, Meara's profiling system provides us with a viable tool which gives a quantifiable measure-ment of text which will enable us to compare texts and text types with each other.

There are a number of measures of lexical content commonly found in the literature, such as lexical density and lexical variety, but they do not directly address the question of the difficulty of a text for a non-native speaker. Indeed as Malvern & Richards (this volume) assert, there are even doubts about the viability of these long-standing and familiar measurements.

As a discipline, ESP has always identified technical vocabulary as a learning area for non-native speakers but the terms 'technical', 'non-technical' and even 'semi-technical' English lack satisfactory definitions. Indeed, there is no agree-ment on what words an expression such as 'semi-technical English' includes; different authors can and do include different words in this category (see, for example, Farrell, 1990). The question of the difficulty or the technicality of language is not an abstract or purely academic one. It is important, for example, where teachers or course writers are trying to match learners of a particular level with appropriate teaching material. What is needed is some indication, a measurement or a profile, which will indicate to us just how difficult or technical a text is. But where even definitions of these qualities are lacking, how is such a thing to be achieved?

The Autohall Project

Between 1992 and 1995 the Centre for Applied Language Studies in Swansea was involved in a project to produce a CD-ROM based course for Greek car mechanics. Specifically, course was to enable the mechanics to read the Nissan technical manual in English: this text provided us with a corpus of nearly 100,000 words. The prospective students had high school English.

Authors have highlighted some features of what might be termed 'work-embedded reading' (Roe, 1993). In certain circumstances, one of the characteristics of this kind of reading is the need for accuracy in interpreting what is said. Hales (1996) points to the example of those working in the finance industry, and it could also be said that in the case of mechanics working on safety-critical parts of a car that the 'educated guessing' of the psycholinguistic approach to reading instruction might not suffice. Both of the above authors go on to discuss the extraction of the language of a 'Target Discourse Community' (Swales, 1990) from a corpus, but for the present work we are not looking for that level of detail. We are instead looking at the problem of text technicality and its resulting lexical difficulty.

A First Look at 'features of the text'

We know at an intuitive level that the Nissan technical manual is difficult for the non-specialist – one has only to give it to an educated native speaker to work with: unless this person has the requisite 'inside knowledge' s/he will not succeed in decoding what is written. In Swalesian terms, the reader is not a member of the appropriate Discourse Community. But is this difficulty a product of the technicality of the text alone or are there features which make it linguistically difficult as well? Is the text hard even for someone with the technical knowledge? In what follows, we demonstrate that a traditional analysis of the features of technical text, although useful at this stage, does not provide the generalised overview of the technicality of the language which we are seeking, nor the answers to the question we have just asked.

To avoid talking in the abstract and for ease of reference, a small section is reproduced in Figure 1.

SHAFT SEAL REMOVAL

1. Remove drain plug, thereby draining the oil.

2. Remove clutch hub, pulley and bearing assembly, and coil assembly. Refer to Compressor Clutch for removal.

3. Using snap ring pliers, compress and remove retainer ring.

4. To remove shaft seal seat, proceed as follows:

(1) Plug high and low pressure (discharge and suction) valve openings of compressor with blind caps.

Note: To plug low pressure (suction) valve, use cap to which seal rubber is fitted.

(2) Connect charging hose to refrigerant can. Install Adapter KV994C1552 to other end of charging hose and insert it into hole in middle of blind cap at low pressure (suction) valve side.

(3) Wrap rag around shaft. Apply pressure [196 to 490 kPa (1.96 to 4.90 bar, 2 to 5 kg/cm, 28 to 71 psi)] from suction side and receive shaft seal seat with rag.

Figure 1 Extract from *Autohall*

Some features stand out as being 'unusual' or 'non-standard', for example:

(1) There is a lack of articles

In the section above there is one definite article and there are no indefinite articles. Indeed, when we come to look at the wordlist in order of frequency, an unusual feature is that the definite article is not the most frequent word type in the corpus, occurring less than half the number of times it does in a more general corpus of the same size. This may be seen in Figure 2 where the most frequent *Autohall* vocabulary is compared with frequency values drawn from *The Guardian* newspaper.

(2) There is a tendency to use long noun phrases

It seems that part of the nature of this corpus is a preponderance of phrases referring to specialist parts where the individual words do not seem particularly exotic or technical, but where these words in combination produce something unintelligible to the uninitiated. Thus, *push, rod* and *tube* are not in themselves obviously unusual vocabulary, but the noun phrase *push rod tube* means nothing outside a car repair manual. In Figure 1, terminology in this category includes: *snap ring pliers* and *shaft seal seat*. These phrases can be very long, as in *low pressure (discharge and suction) valve openings*.

(3) The repetition of noun phrases

There is little use of referencing through pronouns, possibly to avoid possible ambiguity. This is a feature which this genre shares with legal writing (see Crystal & Davy, 1969; Danet, 1985). *It* (403 occurrences) and *they* (36) are the only subject pronouns found in *Autohall*. In the corpus taken from *The Guardian, it* (855), *he* (585), *they* (405), *I* (277), *you* (218) and *we* (176) all occur in the 60 most frequently occurring words.

(4) The limited range of verbs used

There is a very limited range of verbs in the corpus and *remove* is the most common content/non-grammatical word in the corpus, followed by *replace*. In one preliminary sample of the text we made, *install, remove* and *replace* accounted for more than half the verbs used.

(5) The relatively frequent use of such structures as:
— Participle and infinitive phrases (often fronted)
  Using snap ring pliers ...
  To remove shaft seal seat ...
— Imperatives

Given the function of the text, this is probably not too surprising and presumably accounts in part for the markedly small number of pronouns.

It is possible to extend this list considerably and, in the manner of Biber & Finegan (1986), we might be able to produce a list of features which distinguishes the text type. In some respects, the text does not appear to be very difficult to deal with from the point of view of preparing students to decode the text. Such a list, however, appears to be a rather disparate collection of information and our aim is very different from that of Biber & Finegan. We wish to find a fairly quick, preferably automated, and efficient way of identifying what kind of text we are dealing with. Producing a detailed inventory of features may tell us much, but this demands an in-depth analysis which is time consuming and is not yet a fully automated process.

A Lexical Profile as a Quantification

We mentioned above that lexis has for some time been a focus in ESP. It seems feasible that a lexical measurement may, if readily obtainable, provide us with the overall picture we are looking for. To get an idea of the lexical content we can look at the wordlist ordered by frequency. For purposes of comparison we have included figures for a similar-sized corpus taken from the pages of *The Guardian* newspaper (Figure 2).

	Autohall		Guardian			Autohall		Guardian	
1	and	3229	The	6718	31	as	393	their	373
2	the	2485	to	3165	32	that	392	who	329
3	to	2407	of	2982	33	at	389	more	328
4	of	1863	a	2490	34	by	370	which	320
5	in	1297	and	2203	35	clutch	357	had	308
6	is	1243	in	2192	36	shaft	357	its	304
7	or	1110	is	1510	37	piston	356	been	295
8	with	952	for	1218	38	front	348	were	282
9	remove	915	that	1105	39	system	346	I	277
10	a	813	on	982	40	air	340	one	274
11	replace	789	it	855	41	switch	313	or	262
12	for	784	was	721	42	pressure	308	than	262
13	oil	757	be	713	43	transmission	304	if	259
14	be	704	as	627	44	rod	301	would	258
15	valve	681	with	603	45	removal	300	there	248
16	check	657	but	597	46	side	296	said	240
17	engine	596	have	593	47	note	294	out	235
18	from	574	by	590	48	out	287	last	234
19	if	572	he	585	49	seal	278	up	231
20	on	568	are	578	50	ring	272	no	220
21	gear	521	at	550	51	sure	268	you	218
22	install	521	has	543	52	spring	266	when	211
23	rear	507	from	482	53	cover	263	about	202
24	When	491	not	475	54	parts	260	into	194
25	not	480	will	453	55	refer	253	after	183
26	bearing	478	his	435	56	lamp	251	now	181
27	assembly	439	an	409	57	gauge	250	year	181
28	it	403	They	405	58	reverse	240	we	176
29	cylinder	400	all	398	59	are	238	says	175
30	brake	397	this	395	60	nut	230	per	174
					61	case	220	people	172

Figure 2 Most frequent words in *Autohall* and *The Guardian*

For those used to looking at such lists, perhaps the first striking feature is that *the* is not the most frequently occurring type in *Autohall*. This confirms the impression we get from our brief selection in Figure 1.

In the technical corpus, content words begin to appear in the 9th position. This appears to be a feature of much specialised text, and is also noted in specialised financial text in Hales (1996). In the more 'general' text from *The Guardian* we find that content words begin to appear around the 60th position. Combined with a very low lexical variety, this might indicate that we are dealing with a restricted vocabulary, which may perhaps be specialised. However, not all of the words are particularly 'difficult' or 'technical', for example, *remove, replace, air* and *oil* are all frequently occurring words which do not appear to be restricted in any obvious way. But some are clearly more specific to the subject matter of car mechanics, for example, *cylinder, clutch, shaft* and *piston.* The answer may well lie in how these words combine, producing more complex lexical items or lexical phrases (Nattinger & DeCarrico, 1992). This is indeed an important question, and an in-depth investigation would almost certainly reveal many interesting features, but again we find ourselves being drawn to a detailed question which, in terms of the sequence of events, should come later in an examination of our corpus. It should be remembered that we are attempting something which produces an overall picture of the text.

The Overall Picture

The profiling system we mentioned at the beginning of this paper produces statistics which can be viewed conveniently as histograms, as in Figure 3. It was produced by using an early version of a program developed by Meara (1993). In the graph we see the distribution of lexical items found in 1,000 words of text taken from technical and non-technical sources. The technical source is *Autohall*, the Nissan technical manual, and the non-technical source is the magazine *Marie Claire.* We are aware of the difficulties of defining exactly what is 'general' text, so we have used as a point of comparison, text which may be considered 'general public reading' without making any claims for the validity of this as a definition of 'General English' or 'Ordinary Text' beyond the purposes of comparison required in this paper. In case the comparison may appear too predictably extreme, figures for *The Guardian* are also included, as it is generally considered to be a quality newspaper which does not make too many concessions in the level of language it uses.

In the histogram we find the categories of Nation's word list (Nation, 1986) on the x axis, and on the y axis, the percentage of the word forms of the text which fall within each of Nation's groups, which are:

    0 = structure and function words

    1 = first thousand most frequent lexical words

    2 = second thousand most frequent lexical words

    3/4 = everything not in previous groups

These texts have the following distribution:

Table 1 Percentages of words in each of Nation's (1986) levels

Nation level	Percentage of word forms in level		
	Marie Claire	The Guardian	Autohall
0	25%	21%	10%
1	50%	38%	35%
2	10%	20%	25%
3/4	15%	21%	30%

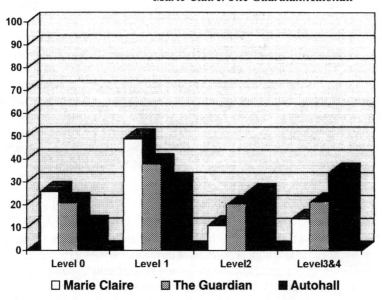

Marie Claire/The Guardian/Autohall

Figure 3 Percentages of words in each of Nation's (1986) levels

Some Observations

The 'ordinary' text (*Marie Claire*) has certain quantifiable features in this profiling system. About 25% of the vocabulary consists of function and structure words and a further 50% of all of the types in the text come from the 1,000 most frequent lexical words in English. A further 10% comes from Nation's level 2 This accounts for some 85% of 'ordinary' text vocabulary. The remainder, about 15%, are the words that fall outside this range, in other words, 15% of 'ordinary' text vocabulary appears to consist of what can be described as infrequent vocabulary. In a more difficult text, *The Guardian*, the balance of vocabulary is different. Text from *The Guardian* contains fewer frequent vocabulary items. About 78% of words in this 1,000 word sample fall within Nation's levels 0, 1 and 2. About 22% thus falls into Nation's level 3. It might be argued, therefore, that one of the linguistic features which makes *The Guardian* more difficult for readers is that it contains proportionately more infrequent vocabulary: roughly 50% more in this sample.

In *Autohall*, we can see that the proportion of frequent vocabulary, in Nation's level 0, 1 and 2, is much smaller than in either *Marie Claire* or *The Guardian*: 67%. In *Autohall*, levels 0 and 1 are very small. Indeed the number of lexical items at level 0 is strikingly small. As a consequence, roughly a third of all words fall within Nation's level 3 and are infrequent vocabulary. This may well be one of the features which marks out technical text from more general text. Technical text contains proportionately more infrequent vocabulary, and the profiling method allows us to quantify this. In the 1,000 word sample, the technical text has twice as much infrequent vocabulary as the general text. If, as is suggested, a high proportion of infrequent vocabulary is a feature of difficult text, then *Autohall* is not merely technical, it is also very difficult. Even though, when dealing with percentages, an increase in one place necessarily leads to a decrease elsewhere, the differences between the two 'ordinary reading' sources and our technical corpus at the extreme levels (0 and 3/4) stand out.

Conclusion

Three important observations have been made in this study. Firstly, the *Autohall* text contains a high proportion of infrequent vocabulary. This identifies it as 'difficult' within this particular definition of 'difficulty', as indicated by the distributions in Figure 3. Secondly, there is an unusual distribution of word types, with a greater proportion of content words and fewer function words than in 'general' text, as partially illustrated in Figure 2. Thirdly, frequent words are collocated in unaccustomed ways, as is clear from Figure 1. This feature of 'technicality' is the one of which a native-speaker could fall foul, by recognising all of the words but still not recognising the message.

Our question in this paper was whether an automated programme that measures 'difficulty' as a function of word frequency distribution can adequately characterise the difficulty of a technical text. The answer to this question must be *no*. The *Autohall* text does contain infrequent words, and these certainly may be seen as a measure of that particular type of 'difficulty'. However, the collocation of frequent words in unusual ways cannot be measured in this way.

A supplementary question also posed at the beginning of the paper was whether a non-native *technician* would have less difficulty understanding the *Autohall* text than (a) a native technician, (b) a non-native technician and (c) a non-native non-technician. Had the word-frequency profiling been sufficient to characterise the text, i.e. had the difficulty of the text resided only in the high proportion of infrequent vocabulary and/or the word-type distributions, then it would have been reasonable to conclude that a non-native technician who knew the infrequent terms in his own language would have an advantage over both native and non-native non-technicians. Furthermore, once familiar with the terminology, he would equal the abilities of the native technician.

However, it appears that the technicality resides additionally in the collocation of frequent words. This makes it less clear whether a non-native technician would find the text easy to handle or not, because strings of words hide semantic and grammatical relations. The reduced number of function words further obscures these relations.

Because of this, we can see that whilst 'difficulty' as a function of word frequency appears to be an independent variable – it would be possible to have a text which had few infrequent words but which was still technical by virtue of its collocations of the frequent ones – the distribution of word-types, specifically the low proportion of function words, contributes to the over-all difficulty of the text in a second way, by obscuring the semantic and grammatical relationships between the frequent words.

So, to what extent can a profiling system based on a model which categorises lexical frequency help us satisfactorily to grade a technical text for overall difficulty? By enabling us to quantify the proportions of frequent and infrequent words, including those of different types, it certainly allows us to produce one indication of the degree of difficulty of the text, and this through a process which can be automated, and therefore speedily implemented. In the real world, this alone may have benefits for teachers and course directors as well as course designers. However, without a component that picks up on the ways in which the frequent vocabulary is used, one major aspect of 'technicality' cannot be measured. Such a component could further help distinguish technical (as opposed to 'difficult') text from a variety of other text types, and possibly help in the definition of what constitutes 'technical' vocabulary and what constitutes 'semi-technical' vocabulary.

This is very much work in progress and there are certainly shortcomings. There is, for example, the requirement to standardise the length of text involved. In this work we have standardised at a level of 1,000 words. This necessarily asks questions of the system's reliability with differing text sizes and the long-standing yet valid question of whether it is viable to use text segments rather than full texts if the text is very long, as it is here (see Sinclair, 1991; Stubbs, 1996). However, the practical benefits mentioned in the previous paragraph seem to make it, for the moment, a workable idea and a promising tool in real-world situations where one might like to reduce the inherent problems of relying on intuition.

We mentioned above that there is an absence of definitions for technical, semi-technical and non-technical vocabulary. In this paper we have demonstrated that such definitions may soon be not only within our grasp, but applicable in an automated screening of texts for learners.

References

Biber, D. and Finegan, E. (1986) An initial typology of English text types. In J. Aarts and W. Meijs (eds) *Corpus Linguistics II* (pp. 19–46). Amsterdam: Editions Rodopi B.V.

Crystal, D. and Davy, D. (1969) *Investigating English Style*. London: Longman.

Danet, B. (1985) Legal discourse. In T. A. Van Dijk (ed.) *Handbook of Discourse Analysis* Vol. 1. New York: Academic Press.

Farrell, P. (1990) *Vocabulary in ESP: A lexical analysis of the English of electronics and a study of semi-technical vocabulary.* Centre for Language and Communication Studies: Occasional Paper No. 25. Dublin: Trinity College.

Hales, T. (1996) Planting seeds: Corpus analysis in reading course production. In *New Directions in Reading: Proceedings of the 1995 Skills Conference.* Cairo: The American University.

Laufer, B and Nation, I. S. P. (1995) Vocabulary Size and Use: Lexical Richness in L2 Written Production. *Applied Linguistics* 16/3, 307–22.

Malvern, D. and Richards, B. (1997) A New Measure of Lexical Density. In A. M. G. Ryan and A. Wray (eds) *Evolving Models of Language.* Multilingual Matters, Clevedon.

Meara (1993) Tintin and the World Service: A look at lexical environments. In 1993 *IATEFL Annual Conference Report Proceedings* (pp. 32–7).

Meara, P., Lightbown, P. M. and Halter, R. H. (1997) Classrooms as lexical environments. *Language Teaching Research* (pp. 28–47).

Nation, I. S. P. (1986) *Word Lists* (revised edn). Victoria, New Zealand: Victoria University English Language Centre.

Nattinger, J. R. and DeCarrico, J. S. (1992) *Lexical Phrases in Language Teaching.* Oxford: Oxford University Press.

Roe, P. (1993) Target language: The Financial Times Proceedings: Second National ESP Seminar. *English for Special Purposes: Applications and implications for human resource development.* Malaysia: Universiti Teknologi.

Sinclair, J. (1991) *Corpus Concordance Collocation.* Oxford: Oxford University Press.

Stubbs, M. (1996) *Text and Corpus Analysis.* Oxford: Blackwell.

Swales, J. (1990) *Genre Analysis: English in academic and research settings.* Cambridge: Cambridge University Press.
Willis, D. (1990) *The Lexical Syllabus.* London: Collins.
Yule, G. (1985) *The Study of Language.* Cambridge: Cambridge University Press.

6 Politeness in Scientific Research Articles Revisited: The use of ethnography and corpus

AKIKO OKAMURA
Newcastle University

Abstract

This study intends to examine insiders' perspectives in scientific discourse. Interviews were conducted with 14 British academics in science and engineering about the use of hedges and their awareness of politeness in writing a research article. The meaning of the term 'politeness' was left to the interpretation of interviewees. Then researchers' responses were analysed within Brown & Levinson's framework of politeness strategies (1987).

The results of interviews showed that professors tend to identify a role for politeness in research articles, while junior researchers tended to deny that there was a role. However when their responses were analysed within Brown & Levinson's framework, the results suggested that they are employing strategies to protect the faces of the writer, the readers and the cited authors.

Since protection of face is the motivation for the use of politeness strategies within Brown & Levinson's framework, politeness does seem to be in operation in research articles.

The interviewees' comments also revealed some limitations of a purely text-based approach. It seems that in order to understand insiders' perspectives in scientific research articles, we need to integrate the ethnographic approach into the text-based approach.

Introduction

It has been argued that hedges in professional scientific research articles are to show politeness while hedges in textbooks show uncertainty (Myers, 1989). Myers (1989) emphasised the role of interaction between the writer and the readers in interpreting the function of hedges. However, recently a study on hedges based on a corpus has suggested that there are few examples of politeness in the corpus of scientific research articles (Hyland, 1996). Since the two studies took different approaches to the analysis of hedges in scientific articles, the differences could be related to this. We need to examine the differences between the two approaches.

Furthermore, as the voices of the writers of the analysed research articles were not directly heard in most previous analyses, we need to observe their perspective on the use of hedges. As scientific research articles are written for the members of a discourse community, it seems crucial to understand a writer's intention behind the linguistic forms he/she uses. Therefore, I attempt to examine through the interviews, writers' perspectives about the use of hedges and the relationship between hedges and politeness in professional discourse. The results are compared to Myers' and Hyland's studies.

Studies of Hedges

Linguistic forms of hedges

Hedging in academic writing has been studied extensively (Crismore & Farnsworth, 1990; Hyland, 1994; Salager-Meyer, 1994, for example) but it has tended to be associated with certain linguistic forms especially modal verbs (Simpson, 1990). In scientific writing the use of hedges indicates a writer's awareness of norms and expectations of the discourse community (Hyland, 1996).

Role of hedges in insiders' communication

Myers (1989) distinguished a difference in terms of interaction patterns between textbooks and research papers; the former is that of insider and outsider while the latter represents the interaction between insiders. He asserts that the hedges in textbooks are to express uncertainty and do not involve politeness. However, hedges in research papers are to show politeness to the academic discourse community as they are employed for interaction among the members of the discourse community (Myers, 1989). Thus Myers (1989) indicates that scientific discourse carries a social dimension behind the impersonal and objective surface. It seems that researchers do not simply let the results speak for themselves, they also manipulate language to persuade readers towards their argument (Thompson, 1994) and show assertion and humility to their professional discourse community (Myers, 1989).

Since Myers' interpretation of politeness is based on Brown & Levinson's politeness strategies (1987), politeness in their terms needs to be clarified.

Politeness theory

Brown & Levinson (1987) described two sets of human 'face wants'. One face represents the wish to be accepted and appreciated – positive face; and the other face concerns the wish not to be disturbed by others – negative face. Since some actions, such as making a request, can be face threatening ('face threatening acts') in order to redress a threat to each face, two types of politeness strategies are employed: one type to protect positive face and the other type to protect negative face. They are called positive and negative politeness strategies respectively. Strategies to show solidarity are considered to be for positive politeness while those for deference and mitigation are for negative politeness.

Recently, this distinction of positive and negative politeness has been questioned (Ide, 1989; Matsumoto, 1988; Meier, 1995). Meier argues that Brown & Levinson's framework tends to pay attention solely to the hearer's face and the distinction may not be a clear dichotomy (1995: 385). By not impeding the hearer, the speaker is acting in accordance with the hearer's wants (Meier, 1995: 385). In order to mitigate impediment, the speaker may use a positive politeness strategy such as appealing to solidarity. Meier concludes that 'any threat to negative face is thus subsumable under positive politeness' (1995: 385).

Emphasising insiders' communication in scientific research articles, Myers' study (1989) opposed hedges to solidarity markers instead of boosters (Holmes, 1995) or strengtheners (House & Kasper, 1981). He gave modal verbs and pronouns as examples of linguistic forms of hedges and solidarity markers as shown below.

Examples:

Solidarity marker:
We as ESP teachers should look for ....   (Myers, 1992: 3)

Hedges:
We wish to suggest a structure for the salt of deoxyribose nucleic acid (D.N.A.). This structure has novel features which are of considerable biological interest. A structure for nucleic acid has already been proposed by Pauling and Correy. They kindly made their manuscript available to us in advance of publication. Their model consists of three intertwined chains, with the phosphates near the fibber axis, and the bases on the outside. In our opinion, this structure is unsatisfactory for two reasons: (...)
                                                    (Watson & Crick, 1953, cited by Myers, 1989: 5)

Although Myers (1989) gives linguistic forms of hedges and solidarity markers, he clearly points out that Brown & Levinson's politeness strategies:

...are not always specific words or phrases that signal politeness: one could not find them just by searching for certain tokens. Rather, politeness is implicated by the semantic structure of the whole utterance. (1989: 22)

The same applies to hedges; although there are certain forms which are strongly associated with hedges such as the modal verbs 'may', 'might', 'can' or 'could', originally hedges were not linked to any linguistic forms (Lakoff, 1972). Hedges can be embedded in context and the semantic structure. Thus in order to identify politeness strategies, we need to understand the context in which particular linguistic forms are employed.

Studies based on a corpus and ethnography

Recently it has become considered essential to have a computer-based corpus in order to analyse the use of language in written texts (Brett, 1994; Thomas & Hawes, 1994; Taylor & Chen, 1991, for example). This approach has provided enormous advantages to the analysis of language use in texts. For example language analysis based on such a corpus can show how lexical items are combined and used by a majority of writers, even though the process is largely outside the writer's conscious control.

However, corpora are not omnipotent tools for the analysis of language use; when there is no one type of realisation of a linguistic device such as hedging, focusing on specific lexical items will not show its full picture. It seems crucial to understand the contextual knowledge shared among the insiders of a discourse community. Lest we miss the demonstration of writer's intention embedded in a text, we need to take the insider's perspective.

Ethnography came originally from anthropology to observe non-European culture with the inhabitants' perspectives rather than with the anthropologists' European perspective. The purpose is to understand the role of their behaviours in their society without judging them against the anthropologists' own cultural norms (Hymes, 1974; Ochs, 1988). It has been applied in ESL to understand classroom activities and the acquisition of second languages (see Watson-Gegeo, 1988). Compared to the approach taken by the studies on corpora, the results are highly context dependent and are not quantitatively oriented. However, they are capable of showing how insiders of the community perceive their individual behaviour and how they perform certain activities in their society.

Hyland (1996) analysed the use of hedging based on his corpus consisting of 26 molecular biology research articles and concluded that 'there is little evidence of politeness in Myers' sense in my corpus' (1996: 258). Although both understood scientific discourse, the two studies seem to be based on different types of approach.

Myers' study is based on his involvement with one scientific discipline, biology. He took an ethnographic approach to the discipline; he refers to the contextual background in each case he quotes (1989, 1990). On the other hand, Hyland's (1996) is a quantitative analysis of linguistic forms which can reveal writers' language use in texts. We need to examine why the two approaches have yielded different understandings of the functions of hedges in scientific research articles.

Since scientific research articles are insider communication, one way to analyse the differences is to interview the writers of research articles.

Purpose of This Study

In order to observe the writers' perspectives, it was decided to explore five aspects of the use of language to realise hedges and politeness in scientific research articles.

(1) Functions of hedging expressions.

(2) Strategies for mitigating criticism of others.

(3) Embedding of hedges in context.

(4) The relationship between the use of modal verbs and politeness.

(5) Scientists' awareness of politeness in scientific discourse.

The second question was intended to examine indirectly the role of politeness in writing a research article. The criticism here refers to negative attitude to the cited work. The third question was about how scientists use shared knowledge among readers to hedge their criticism of others' work. The fourth question concerned the scientists' awareness of the link between one linguistic form and its function. Modal verbs were selected because they have been considered to be related to politeness (Myers, 1989).

Data Collection

Data came from the analysis of 24 scientific research articles and interviews with their authors.

Procedure

First, scientific research articles were collected from 14 British researchers working in the scientific departments at Newcastle University. Ten of the researchers provided the author with copies of two different published research articles, while the rest provided one. Thus altogether 24 research articles were examined. In analysing these, all the modal verbs 'may', 'might', 'could' and 'can' were underlined, and other expressions which refer to previous work were also underlined.

Then the underlined words were divided into two types: one employed to describe the writer's results and the other used to criticise other researchers' work. The method section of the papers was excluded from the analysis because in the method section the analysed papers only refer to previous work as a reference point from which readers can obtain further information. From all the underlined expressions, four to five expressions in each research article were chosen as references for the interview; this choice was to cover various linguistic forms such as modal verbs, adverbs, adjectives, and conditional expressions based on Hyland's analysis of hedges (1996).

In order to examine the use of context (Research question 3), I also underlined expressions where the writers appeared to imply criticism of others' work by using knowledge shared with their readers.

Finally five interview questions were formulated to obtain the writers' perspectives. They were:

(1) What do you mean by this hedging expression here?
(2) If you need to mitigate criticism, what do you do?
(3) Are you criticising previous work here?
(4) What is the role of modal verbs here? Is it related to politeness?
(5) Do you think that there is politeness in science? If so, what would it be?

The interview questions 1, 3, 4 referred to the underlined expressions in the writers' research articles. Criticism here does not include positive and constructive critical comments. It only refers to negative criticism.

Each interview lasted approximately 45 to 60 minutes and took place mostly in interviewees' offices except on two occasions when the interviewer's office was more conveniently located. The interviews were recorded and transcribed by me.

Subjects (interviewees – the writers of analysed research articles)

Field	Academic position
Microbiology	2 professors
Civil engineering	1 professor and 2 researchers
Physiology	1 professor
Medicine (respiratory)	1 researcher
Chemistry	2 professors
Biology	1 professor and 3 senior lecturers
Soil science	1 senior lecturer

Eleven of these researchers (senior lecturers and professors) have experience of being a reviewer and most of them have served on the editorial board of an international journal.

Results

The functions of hedging type

Two questions were asked about the writer's intention in the use of hedging expressions in their articles. As explained in the table on p. 89, hedging expressions were divided into two types (type 1 is employed for the description of own results and type 2 is for criticism of others' work).

When asked the reasons for the use of type 1 hedges, all the researchers responded that they were uncertain or they intended to be cautious about their interpretation of the results.

One researcher commented that a scientific claim has truth value only if certain conditions are met. Thus whatever the claim is, it always needs to carry hedging expressions as it is only valid in a given context. As Hyland (1996) pointed out, hedges are an essential element in scientific discourse.

For the function of type 2 hedges, it might be assumed that writers use hedges to avoid direct confrontation, as is the case in everyday conversation. However, all the researchers explained that they hedged because they were not certain and that it was nothing to do with politeness. Three researchers also added that they hedged because they did not have sufficiently strong backing evidence to be critical. Expectations of the research community do not allow writers to be critical if they cannot provide strong evidence to support their argument (Hyland, 1996).

Strategies for criticism and mitigation

The relationship between hedging and politeness was explored. Most of the researchers stated that in criticising previous work, they would clarify the reason why they do not agree with other researchers' work.

Also, researchers gave several strategies they normally use to mitigate criticism in their research articles. Some researchers pointed out that they would avoid strong words, use impersonal expressions or contact the criticised researcher for his/her opinion before the paper appeared in print. These strategies seem to be related to politeness strategies within the framework of Brown & Levinson's term (1987). As politeness refers to the employment of strategies to redress a threat to face (see p. 86), we need to consider whose face is threatened in writing a research article.

The researchers' responses can be categorised into two types: one type is intended to protect one's own face and the other is intended to protect the cited author's face as shown in Figure 1.

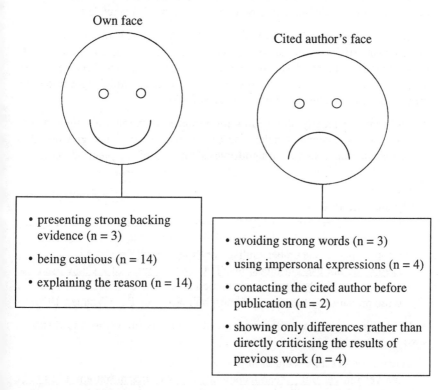

Figure 1 Use of strategies to criticise others' work in scientific research articles

From the responses shown in Figure 1, we can observe how researchers protect their own and cited authors' face wants. The researchers seem to attempt to maintain their scientific rigour to protect their own face and at the same time to act in a socially appropriate way to protect the cited author's face. Since the interaction is happening in public, i.e. in print, they need to keep their credibility in the professional community by the use of various strategies.

Previously analyses have tended to represent readers as a whole (Myers, 1989). However, as the researchers' responses suggest that they are aware of the cited authors, the analysis of the interaction with the cited authors may create a new dimension to the analysis of politeness in scientific research articles. This will be discussed later.

Hedges embedded in context

Obviously contextual knowledge is crucial to understanding a writer's claims in scientific research articles. What we need is to examine how a writer makes the best use of knowledge shared between the writer and the readers.

Contextual knowledge can make the writer's implicit intention clear to insiders; superficially critical comments may not be as critical as they seem to outsiders if they are interpreted in context. Therefore, the researchers were asked whether they were in fact criticising authors in passages which appeared to be critical to me as an outsider (Interview question 3).

One example clearly shows how the writer's intention was embedded in context. Without contextual understanding, linguistic forms below give outsiders to the field an impression of straightforward criticism of one piece of work.

Example 1:

The analysed text:
Koostra and Harrington (1969) reported an increase in LPC in ageing cucumber seeds and did not report PA. In contrast, we did not find any lysopholipids in cucumber. Unlike our experiments, Koostra and Harrington (1969) did not use 2-dimensional TLC. What source of PA they used was not indicated in their report: synthetic PA may have different Rf values to those prepared by the action of phospholipase D on PC. (Wuthier, 1976)

However, when the writer was asked about his intention, his response was:

Interviewee (a senior lecturer in plant biology):
um yes um yes but I mean technically it is a criticism but um it has to be understood in the context that um they published in 1969 it was the first paper on this topic (right) ..it was an important paper and and you know you will not get everything right first time.. it's inevitable.. it's not really a criticism of the past it's just it's just…and I don't know that we always successfully distinguish that from the situation where we really are criticising it ....

It seems that we need to consider the historical background as perceived by members of the discourse community. Although in this instance the researcher interviewed might be hedging himself about his writing, it is possible to suggest that linguistic analysis alone may not reveal the writer's strategic use of contextual clues. This indicates that we need to consider contextual knowledge. The ethnographic approach can yield insight into insiders' interaction in discourse, as in Myers' studies (1989, 1990), where a corpus approach alone cannot do so.

The role of modal verbs in relation to politeness

The following example summarises most of the researchers' responses about the relationship between modal verbs and politeness.

Example 2:

Interviewee (a senior lecturer in biology):

> no..I don't think it's like in Japanese way you say politeness.. I think it's a cautiousness it's essentially rather being polite it's just being …it's hedging your bets really if you are not totally convinced about something it just gives you a enough leeway…say I've never said it dogmatically I just said you know it might be as it were.

It seems that politeness does not seem to be a major factor in the selection of modal verbs, which is in line with Hyland's study (1996).

However, although most of the researchers maintained that the modal verbs 'may', 'might', 'can' and 'could' were used to show uncertainty and cautiousness as described above, three senior researchers gave another view on the use of modals, when asked about the function of modal verbs.

One example is:

Example 3:

Interviewer:

> somebody said that when they say in science 'this could be the case', 'could' is not to do with uncertainty it's to do with humility.. is that true?

Interviewee (a professor in biology):

> yes..

Interviewer:

> when you use 'could' or 'would' or 'may' is it to do with humility rather than uncertainty?

Interviewee:

> it is both it is both.. but it is more to do with with humility than uncertainty.. if you thought something through and you reached conclusion and you think that it fits then you want to say this fits no this looks as though it's right but everybody knows from their experience over the years you can't there's no way you can guarantee you thought of all the problems all the difficulties that might occur and so the only sensible thing is to say this might be right and the other side is this this question of humility but it is a fact of you know human nature that people respond to humility with acceptance whereas they respond to arrogance with rejection ....

Humility is one of the politeness strategies within the Brown & Levinson framework of politeness (1987), where politeness is employed to redress a threat to face. Thus the comments in Example 3 suggest the close relationship between modal verbs and one politeness strategy (Myers, 1989). It seems that politeness strategies are at work in scientific research articles, although this tended to be the perspective provided by the more senior researchers. It was much more difficult to get across the meaning of the question to junior researchers. Some researchers were baffled by my question and tried to explain the essence of scientific discipline. The professor in Example 3 used the words 'everybody knows from their experience over the years'; experience in the field plays a role in judging the strength of claim to be made in the field and how to present it in such a way as to be accepted by the discourse community. At junior level, researchers can be aware of the humility needed when making scientific assertions but may not associate it with a strategy to negotiate strength of claim with the fellow members of a discourse community.

Researchers' awareness of politeness in scientific research articles

The meaning of the term 'politeness' was not defined and it was left to the interpretation of researchers. The intention was to interpret the researchers' comments in terms of Brown & Levinson's politeness framework later. As science is perceived as persuading readers with objective and logical force rather than with politeness, obviously this was the most difficult question to ask scientists. So there was always a long pause when this question was asked.

However, it was again the more experienced senior researchers who acknowledged politeness as an element to consider in writing a research article. Four of the senior researchers recognised its role in science while the other interviewees tended to not to do so.

Sometimes other researchers acknowledged its role later, in the process of discussing it. An interview with one senior lecturer was a case in point. It seems that scientists were not aware of politeness but subconsciously they were employing certain politeness strategies as the following extract reveals:

Example 4:

Interviewer:

and so if there is such a thing as politeness.... because it's a human interaction in a way..when you refer to somebody.. you may need to criticise somebody..

Interviewee (a senior lecturer in soil science):

no I don't think I don't think I don't think politeness is is is I don't think that really comes to my mind really you are wanting to be honest and open and straightforward and say you know we disagree we find the results that disagree with somebody else ur ur our interpretation and what they found are different um and obviously there are occasions when there are disputes and people will be criticised and they will be upset and they will write ur and they will you know they wish to have their view made and so so that you will see in the literature letters to the editor that are published and there are little discussions where people have disagreed and so on people have been criticised and they say we have been unfairly criticised um .... I think the the editor would occasionally have to be um...... I think you could use language which was impolite... I think it's possible to be impolite ur ....you know by by saying by being um..you know by being so critical um that that it becomes impolite ....so <u>perhaps it's true to say that politeness does enter into......now that you make me discuss it and think about it.. yes... yeah...</u>

The former perspective can be seen in the following example.

Example 5:

Interviewee (a professor in physiology):

I think that I think that politeness in science... it's not ... it's um ..(pause) politeness in science in writing a scientific paper is about respect..the amount you can claim in the paper (I see..) for the amount you can claim actually claim in the paper...so that you know however good your data.. um there's a limit to what you can claim for it and I think that generally speaking you <u>you got to show humility..</u>(humbleness) yes in writing now because you know any scientific paper has a limited perspective and you are looking at a very small thing and so that humility is that all this being done before so in another words you have to recognise all the work which has been done previously that's the politeness you mustn't miss anybody out.. <u>you must be fair to everybody in the citation</u> and describing work you are able to build your work and you then put your data you must claim what you can claim ....

The above professor's comments on politeness in writing a scientific research article showed one more face to protect, i.e. the cited author's face. On p. 90 it was shown that in writing a research article, the researcher intends to protect his/her own face and the cited authors' faces by using politeness strategies. The comments in Example 5 above reveal the existence of two types of interaction: interaction with readers in general and interaction with cited authors. Humility was employed for the interaction with the members of the discourse community who were the readers of his article. Fair citation was employed for the interaction with the cited authors.

These two types can be described in Figure 2:

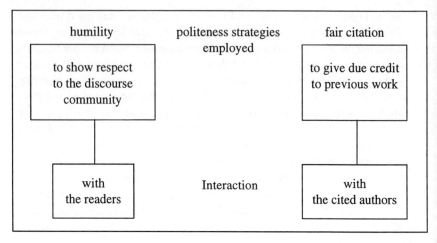

Figure 2

Combined with the results shown on p. 90, the researchers' responses suggest that through the use of politeness strategies, the writer tries to protect the faces of the writer, the readers and the cited authors.

Senior researchers explained that although the editor and referees are there to maintain a certain amount of politeness in research articles, politeness was often violated. In particular, the interviewed researchers pointed out that they sometimes see unfair citation, i.e. deliberately ignoring certain work as shown below.

Example 6:

Interviewer:
   when it comes to citation..when you have rivals working in the same area, do you cite them...

Interviewee (a professor in chemistry):
   yes I mean we we usually try to um you know cite papers that are published by our rivals as much as we have to...really you know ..there's specific papers but we we we like to mention our papers maybe slightly more than competitors' papers and I think yes certainly Japanese cite papers ok most of most of Europe except French....the French just don't um they are chauvinistic you know they um like to just have their..they just absolutely don't do it unless they have to do it..um many citations that are appearing in papers from our rivals in France I mean they are inserted when I get papers to referee then I say what about this you must cite this and this .. if I don't get a paper to referee then we don't see reference to our work so this.. French yes are like that...they don't like to they like to invent everything themselves.. they don't want to use other people's results if they can help it...

It seems that although strong words of criticism can be easily pointed out, it might be the case that researchers' deliberate avoidance of citing other's work sometimes escape the editor's or referees' attention.

Discussion

Exoteric and two types of esoteric audience

Previously Myers (1989) explained the roles of exoteric audience and esoteric audience; the former is to refer to those who are interested in science in general, while the latter means researchers in the field.

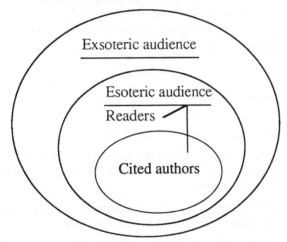

Figure 3

As was shown in the results of the interviews (see pp. 90 and 94), the esoteric audience can be further categorised into the readers and the cited authors as shown in Figure 3. It is therefore necessary to consider the writer's strategies to protect the cited author's face in staking a new knowledge claim in a discourse community.

The role of politeness in scientific research articles

The researchers tended to believe that politeness was not the motivation for the use of hedges when making claims or criticising others' work. They tended to assert that hedging expressions were for uncertainty and to show caution in their interpretation of the results; this agrees with the conclusions of Hyland (1996).

Researchers' responses to the use of hedges, politeness and modal verbs were also analysed within the Brown & Levinson framework. The results suggested that researchers are in fact employing politeness strategies to protect face. The results have shown that writers intend to protect three types of face in constructing argument in scientific research articles: writer's face, cited author's face and reader's face. In Brown & Levinson's terms, politeness seems to be working in scientific research articles.

The role of context in scientific research articles

The results of the current study have shown that contextual knowledge and experience in the field play a crucial role in understanding the roles of hedges and politeness in research articles. This suggests that in order to gain a full picture of scientific discourse, it may not be enough to rely on the analysis of linguistic forms without examining insiders' perspectives. It seems that politeness is not something that researchers can easily spot in a text, but that it is intricately embedded in the semantic structure.

Conclusion

Importance of the two approaches in understanding scientific discourse

This study has drawn on both the corpus-based approach of Hyland (1996) and the ethnographic approach of Myers (1989, 1990).

The writer's intention hidden in context seem to account for the different conclusions drawn by Myers (1989) and Hyland (1996) towards the function of hedges in scientific research articles.

Linguistic analysis based on a large corpus provides enormous insights into the use of language employed by writers. However, this study suggests some limitation of purely text-based analysis. In particular, since the analysis of scientific discourse requires the understanding of the implicit meaning in texts, it is essential to examine insiders' perspectives. A combination of the two approaches would then appear to be beneficial.

This study only touches on small number of researchers within a limited number of disciplines. Thus further study is necessary to expand our understanding of insiders' perspective of the use of linguistic forms and their functions in scientific research articles.

Acknowledgements

Many thanks are due to all the interviewed researchers for their co-operation, Dr Hugh Gosden and my supervisor Dr Philip Shaw for insightful comments and warm support, and Jean Crocker for English correction.

References

Brett, P. (1994) A genre analysis of the results section of sociology articles. *English for Specific Purposes* 13, 47–59.

Brown, P. and Levinson, S. (1987) *Politeness: Some universals in language usage.* Cambridge: Cambridge University Press.
Crismore, A. and Farnsworth, R. (1990) Metadiscourse in popular and professional science discourse. In W. Nash (ed.) *The Writing Scholar: Studies in academic discourse* (pp. 95–117). Newbury Park, CA: Sage.
Holmes, J. (1995) *Women, Men, and Politeness.* London/New York: Longman.
House, J. and Kasper, G (1981) Politeness markers in English and German. In Florian Coulmas (ed.) *Conversational Routine* (pp. 157–85). The Hague: Mouton.
Hyland, K. (1994) Hedging in academic writing and EAP textbooks. *English for Specific Purposes* 13, 239–56.
— (1996) Talking to the academy: Forms of hedging in science research articles.*Written Communication* 13, 251–81.
Hymes, D. (1974) Toward ethnographies of communication. In *Foundations in Sociolinguistics: An ethnographic approach* (pp. 3–28). Philadelphia: University of Pennsylvania Press.
Ide, S. (1989) Formal forms and discernment: Two neglected aspects of linguistic politeness. *Multilingua* 8, 223–48.
Lakoff, G. (1972) Hedges: A study in meaning criteria and the logic of fuzzy concepts. *Chicago Linguistic Society Papers* 8, 183–228.
Matsumoto, Y. (1988) Reexamination of face. *Journal of Pragmatics* 12, 403–26.
Meier, A. J. (1995) Passage of politeness. *Journal of Pragmatics* 24, 381–92.
Myers, G. (1989) The pragmatics of politeness in scientific articles. *Applied Linguistics* 10, 1–35.
— (1990) *Writing Biology.* Madison, WI: University of Wisconsin Press.
— (1992) Textbooks and the sociology of scientific knowledge. *English for Specific Purposes* 11, 3–17.
Ochs, E. (1988) *Culture and Language Development.* Cambridge: Cambridge University Press.
Salager-Meyer, F. (1994) Hedges and textual communicative function in medical English written discourse. *English for Specific Purposes* 13, 149–71.
Simpson, P. (1990) Modality in Literary-Critical Discourse. In W. Nash (ed.) *The Writing Scholar: Studies in academic discourse* (pp. 63–94). Newbury Park: Sage.
Taylor, G. and Chen T. (1991) Linguistic, cultural, and subcultural issues in contrastive discourse analysis: Anglo-American and Chinese scientific text. *Applied Linguistics* 12, 319–36.
Thomas, S. and Hawes, T. P. (1994) Reporting verbs in medical journal articles. *English for Specific Purposes* 13, 129–48.
Thompson, D. K. (1994) Arguing for Experimental 'Facts' in Science. *Written Communication* 10, 106–28.
Watson-Gegeo, K. A. (1988) Ethnography in ESL: Defining the essentials. *TESOL Quarterly* 22, 575–92.

7 Whorf's Children: Critical comments on Critical Discourse Analysis (CDA)

MICHAEL STUBBS
FB2 Anglistik, Universität Trier, Germany

Abstract

CDA has been a frequent topic at BAAL and AILA. Yet one critic, basically sympathetic (Stubbs, 1994), comments on 'major unresolved criticisms of its data and theory', while another, much less sympathetic (Widdowson, 1995a,b, 1996), argues that CDA involves basic conceptual confusions. Benjamin Lee Whorf posed a still unresolved question: do diverse languages influence the habitual thought of their speakers? CDA shifts this question to different patterns of use within a single language, but it makes no clear claim as to how language use might affect habitual thought. Studies of language use and cognition must be comparative: but CDA provides no systematic comparisons between texts and norms in the language. Also, language and thought can only be related if one has data and theory pertinent to both: otherwise the theory is circular. This paper discusses, not entirely optimistically, whether CDA can be rescued from circularity. Via brief case studies, it illustrates how individual texts can be studied against an intertextual background of normative data from large historical and contemporary corpora, the discourse of likely readers of the texts, and a sociohistorical analysis of the dissemination and reception of texts.

Introduction

A model of language which has evolved very fast in the 1990s is an approach to textual commentary known as critical discourse analysis (CDA). In a period of only a few years, it has become very influential, and has been the subject of many papers, including plenaries, at both BAAL and AILA.

Although, in this paper, I make several criticisms of CDA, I hope my comments will be taken in a positive spirit. Many of the observations made in CDA seem to me to be correct. I think, however, that the analyses could be strengthened by comparative and quantitative methods, and that the logic of the position could be better argued.

Definition

It is because CDA raises important social issues, that it is worthwhile trying to strengthen its analyses. CDA argues that there are relations between language, power and ideology, and between how the world is represented in texts and how people think about the world. The following definitions cover several essential points:

> Critical Discourse Analysts [...] feel that it is [...] part of their professional role to investigate, reveal and clarify how power and discriminatory value are inscribed in and mediated through the linguistic system: Critical Discourse Analysis is essentially political in intent. (Caldas-Coulthard & Coulthard, 1996: xi)

> Critical linguistics [...] formulated an analysis of public discourse, an analysis designed to get at the ideology coded implicitly behind the overt propositions [...] Critical linguistics insists that all representation is mediated, moulded by the value systems that are ingrained in the medium [...] The proponents [...] are concerned to use linguistic analysis to expose misrepresentation [...] the critical linguist is crucially concerned with the relativity of representation. (Fowler, 1996: 3, 4, 10)

Key concepts include: representation, mediation, implicit or hidden meanings, and the explicitly political aim of analysing power and inequality, not just to interpret the world but to change the world. In addition to this critique of ideology, important themes are the relation between changes in discourse and wider socio-cultural change, and the claim that language has acquired new functions in the late-modern world (Fairclough, 1992). However, the two themes are closely connected, since they both concern relations between ways of talking and ways of thinking, and I will here treat them together.

I will take as representative two books which have the phrase 'critical discourse analysis' in the title (Fairclough, 1995a; Caldas-Coulthard & Coulthard, 1996) and four other books by Fairclough (1989, 1992, 1995a,b). Also relevant is work by Fowler (1991a), Hodge & Kress (1988, 1993), Kress (1990) and Meinhof & Richardson (1994). Caldas-Coulthard & Coulthard (1996: xi) regard 'the leading names in the field' to be Fairclough, Fowler, Kress, van Dijk, van Leeuven, and Wodak.

Criticisms

CDA aims to provide social criticism which is based on firm linguistic evidence: both politically committed and grounded in 'systematic and detailed textual analysis' (Fairclough, 1995a: 187). However, I will question the extent to which CDA meets 'standards of careful, rigorous and systematic analysis' (Fairclough & Wodak, 1997: 259). I will mostly formulate my criticisms as a series of questions, since I think that some of them can be answered. However, the paper is not entirely optimistic, and I will argue that CDA is unavoidably circular in certain respects.

Some sharp criticisms have been around for a long time, but remain unanswered. A repeated criticism is that the textual interpretations of critical linguists are politically rather than linguistically motivated, and that analysts find what they expect to find, whether absences or presences. Sharrock & Anderson (1981) are ironic with reference to critical linguists such as Kress and Fowler:

> [O]ne of the stock techniques employed by Kress and his colleagues is to look in the wrong place for something, then complain that they can't find it, and suggest that it is being concealed from them. (p. 291)

Amongst many criticisms, Widdowson (1995a,b, 1996) also criticises CDA for a political agenda which is not clearly grounded in linguistic analysis, and he is severe in his overall characterisations of Fairclough (1992):

> [...] essentially sociological or socio-political rather than linguistic [...] an impressive display of apparent scholarship [...] profligate with terms whose conceptual significance is uncertain [...] interpretation in support of belief takes precedence over analysis in support of theory [...] perhaps conviction counts for more than cogency. (Widdowson, 1995b)

Perhaps particularly significant are criticisms by Fowler (1996: 8, 12), one of the originators of critical linguistics:

> [M]ajor problems remain with critical linguistics [...] [D]emonstrations [tend] to be fragmentary, exemplificatory, and they usually take too much for granted in the way of method and of context. [...] [N]owadays it seems that anything can count as discourse analysis [...] [T]here is a danger [of] competing and uncontrolled methodologies drawn from a scatter of different models in the social sciences.

These quotations express several fundamental criticisms: that CDA's methods of data collection and text analysis are inexplicit, that the data are often restricted to text fragments, and that it is conceptually circular, in so far as its own interpretations of texts are as historically bound as anyone else's, and that it is a disguised form of political correctness.

For other criticisms, see Candlin's introduction to Fairclough (1995a: viii–ix) on theoretical and methodological problems, and Hammersley (1996) on problems with CDA's relation to 'critical theory'. In a more sympathetic overview, Richardson (1987) points to problems with the frequent metaphors of visibility and concealment.

The Essential Questions

I will concentrate on questions of data, description and theory. The first is:

Q1. By what criteria can CDA's textual analyses be evaluated?

How does CDA stand up to evaluation against standard criteria such as the explicitness and testability of underlying hypotheses, the replicability of methods of analysis and the reliability of results (such that different analysts would produce the same analysis), comprehensive coverage of data, and representativeness of data?

In particular, CDA never explicitly answers the question of what relation is claimed between formal features of texts and their interpretation. Indeed, I think contradictory views are taken. On the one hand, both Fairclough (1989: 110ff) and Fowler (1991a: 66ff) provide lists of formal linguistic features which are likely to be ideologically significant, and such features are cited in analyses. On the other hand, both Fairclough (1995a: 71) and Fowler (1991b: 90, 1996: 9) emphasise that ideology cannot be read off texts in a mechanical way, since there is no one-to-one correspondence between forms and functions.

On the one hand, a text is seen as a series of traces left by the processes of production. On the other hand, these traces may be ambiguous. A commonly cited example is that an agentless passive has no self-evident ideological reading: it may be used manipulatively to conceal human agency, but it may be used because the human agent is irrelevant, or obvious to everyone from background knowledge, or already known because previously mentioned in the text, or it may simply be used to make the sentence shorter.

Therefore CDA's descriptive claims are often unclear. In any case, if it is not possible to read the ideology off the texts, then the analysts themselves are reading meanings into texts on the basis of their own unexplicated knowledge. (The circularity problem.)

This question can be formulated from the point of view of the text itself or the readers of the text. Fowler (1996: 7) points out that in much (all?) work in CDA, 'the reader simply is not theorized'. So an alternative formulation of question 1 is:

Q2. What source of interpretative authority does CDA claim?

CDA warns us that there are no brute facts and no disinterested texts, and emphasises the force of history and of one's point of view. But if there are no disinterested texts, it follows that CDA is not itself immune to these points, and that its own interpretations also embody interests. The fact that this is noted from time to time by practitioners does not get CDA out of this particular Catch 22. We cannot have it both ways.

I move now to more specific descriptive claims.

Q3. What descriptive claim is being made about mixed texts?

In the context of an argument that changing ways of talking are inherently related to wider processes of cultural change, Fairclough (e.g. 1995a: 142ff, 192ff) observes that many texts are hybrids: for example, both academic writing and political debates on television are becoming more colloquial. It is a common observation that public language in general (including much written academic language) is becoming less formal, that many texts (for example, in advertising) are heterogeneous, and that such mixing is a statistical phenomenon (Coseriu, 1988: 26ff).

However, Fairclough makes no precise descriptive claims in this area. He points to a phenomenon which is essentially quantitative, but provides no quantitative findings for individual texts, no comparisons between different texts or text types, no quantitative diachronic findings that textual heterogeneity is increasing, and indeed no methods for calculating heterogeneity in texts. A claim is made about a probabilistic phenomenon, but no refutable findings or methods are provided.

Like many approaches to stylistic variation, CDA has a strong tendency either to analyse just a few stylistic features (sometimes a single word, such as enterprise: see Fairclough, 1995a: 112), or to conceive of stylistic variation in terms of simple dichotomies, such as public and private, or homogeneous and heterogeneous. Yet it is well known that registers are very rarely defined by individual features, but consist of clusters of associated features which have a greater than chance tendency to co-occur: such a concept is argued in great empirical detail by Biber (1988, 1995). This view of register variation is essential to the Hallidayan perspective often cited within CDA.

These points leave us with the question of exactly what link is being claimed between ways of talking and ways of thinking. So, the next question involves the essential theoretical claim made in CDA.

Q4. What relation is claimed between language use and cognition?

CDA discusses both how discourse is shaped by power and ideologies, and also how discourse has an effect on social identities and systems of belief. Language use is both 'socially shaped and socially constitutive' (Fairclough, 1995a: 131, and elsewhere). Given this dialectic, it is all the more difficult to state what relations are being claimed. In Fairclough (1995a), the topic under discussion is clear enough in a general way – the micro-macro links between language use and social institutions – and this topic can be seen from such quotes as the following:

'language in its relation to power and ideology' (p. 1)

'discourse has taken on a major role in sociocultural reproduction' (p. 2)

'texts are social spaces in which two fundamental social processes simultaneously occur: cognition and representation of the world, and social interaction' (p. 6)

'texts [are] sensitive indicators of sociocultural processes and change' (p. 8)

'discourse conventions are a most effective mechanism for sustaining hegemonies' (p. 91)

So much is clear. But I am not clear what precise meaning is to be given to terms such as relations, role, processes, indicators and mechanism. CDA aims to be a theory of the relation between cognition and the textual representation of reality. But I am uncertain about the extent to which cause and effect relations are being claimed, about the nature of evidence which textual traces are said to provide of social change, and so on. Briefly, I am not convinced that CDA provides testable claims about such relations.

There are two more precise sub-questions which I am sure CDA does not answer:

Q5. How does language use actually affect habitual thought?

CDA is a theory of how things come to be taken for granted. A constant argument is that many of our beliefs and representations might seem simply natural, but they are naturalised. But CDA is vague about the actual mechanisms whereby such influences operate. An even more concrete sub-question is:

Q6. How does frequency of use relate to naturalisation?

CDA presents no theory about the role of repetition in such influences. In common with linguistics in general, it has no theory of how our ways of seeing the world are influenced cumulatively by repeated phrasings in texts. Exactly what is the relation between frequency of use and cognition?

All studies in this area have to address the severe logical problem of potential circularity, so the next question is:

Q7. Can CDA escape from circular language-cognition claims?

The empirical question is: What non-linguistic evidence of cognition is provided? I have already cited Sharrock & Anderson's (1981) arguments that a basic aim of critical linguistics is to determine what is revealed or concealed in a text, but that much work is circular, because analysts 'know perfectly well at the outset' just what political position they are going to find.

So how could circularity be avoided? The basic claim of CDA (and of Whorfian views) is that languages or uses of language implicitly classify experience, and that these categories influence a person's view of reality. There is therefore an essential criterion for any research. There must be non-linguistic evidence of a pattern of beliefs and behaviour. If language and thought are to be related, then one needs data and theory pertinent to both. If we have no independent evidence, but infer beliefs from language use, then the theory is circular. This may be the most difficult type of evidence to provide, but there is no way around this demand, especially in light of the constant claim in CDA that certain meanings are hidden from speakers and hearers, and can be revealed only by certain types of analysis.

Although it is frequently emphasised that, as well as the texts themselves, one should study 'how texts are produced, distributed and consumed' (Fairclough, 1995a: 1), CDA fails here to meet its own criterion. So a variant of Question 7 is:

Q8. What are the relations between text, addressor and addressee?

Audience reception work is common in media studies, but not in CDA. Note again, that the question of two possible sources of interpretative authority, text and audience, is not tackled by CDA itself.

The criterion that one should study text production and consumption could be met only by ethnographic studies of social institutions. Some such studies are available outside CDA. For example, Bell (1991) has studied, not only as a linguist but as a working journalist, the interactive processes which lie behind the production of newspaper texts. News media offer 'the classic case of language produced by multiple parties' (p. 33), in which journalist, editor and sub-editor all handle a text and modify its language, cutting, reordering, and rewriting in accordance with a house style, and providing links, visuals and headlines. When a locally authored news story is transmitted internationally via news agencies such as Reuters, then the multiple-author production process is even more complex.

Q9. How can comparative studies be designed?

Since the essential claim concerns differences caused by different language use, it follows that studies of language use and cognition must be comparative. Only very few CDA studies compare individual texts, or compare features of texts with norms in the language, or compare text types diachronically. These are all cases where it is not too difficult to see how such gaps could be filled. For example, Krishnamurty (1996) studies both individual texts and also data from different large corpora, totalling some 140 million running words, to investigate the assumptions underlying the words ethnic, racial and tribal. And Fairclough & Mauranen (in press) compare extracts from political television interviews in English and Finnish.

One can also reformulate these questions from the point of view of data.

Q10. How are data selected? Are they representative?

In its simplest formulation, the criticism here is that not much data is analysed. More generally, there is very little discussion of whether it is adequate to restrict analysis to short fragments of data, how data should be sampled, and whether the sample is representative. Often data fragments are presented with no justification at all that they are representative. However, consider the following case in which questionable claims to representativeness are made.

Meinhof & Richardson (1994) present articles which analyse how poverty is portrayed in a corpus of British media texts. (The book appears in a series which takes 'a critical approach' to language, society and social change.) The texts, from newspapers and television, were sampled from ten days in 1991. This period was chosen in advance: that is, the sample was arbitrary or random, in the sense that the authors could not have known in advance what the data would contain. However, the editors (p. 5) claim that it is a 'representative sample'. It clearly isn't, and indeed they point out themselves why it isn't: in these ten days, there was no 'central trigger event which would have put poverty on the national agenda' (p. 4). That is, had there been some such event (perhaps a government report; or an elderly person, living alone, found dead by neighbours), then the reporting would have been different. In fact, they say (p. 5) that they were 'more interested in the everyday, mundane coverage of poverty', and therefore imply that they would have rejected the data if it had – by chance – included such a trigger event. At any rate, their sample is arguably random, but does not represent the range of variation one might expect in media coverage of poverty.

With reference to questions 9 and 10, there are studies which look historically and comparatively at relatively large data sets. Examples include van Noppen (1996) on a large corpus of Methodist discourse from the 1700s, Ehlich (1989) on fascist discourse in Germany, and Wodak (1996) on racist discourse in Austria. The question still arises, however, of the sense in which the data fragments cited in individual articles illustrate or represent the larger corpus.

An additional problem of data presentation arises with some work which is done on translated texts. One view might be that presenting data only in translation is an extreme form of decontextualisation, which means that readers who have no access to the original language must put up with a severe loss of information. For example, Wodak (1996: 111) cites the phrase, in English only, *hostility to foreigners.* But this notion happens not to be lexicalised in this way in English. The phrase is obviously a translation of one of two common German compound words: *Fremdenhass* or *Ausländerfeindlichkeit.* On the other hand, if analysis is in fact possible using only translated texts, then this implies that fine details of the text are, after all, not relevant to ideological analysis. Compare the problem of Whorf arguing that Hopi grammar embodies a world-view, but then explaining perfectly clearly – in English – what this world-view is. Again the conclusion seems to be that CDA is uncertain about which features of language use (words? discourse structure? repetition?) have an effect on habitual thought.

Questions about language and ideology are of course asked not only within CDA, and much work needs to be done to locate CDA within a broad tradition of work on the social construction of reality. So my final main question is:

Q11. How does CDA relate to other constructivist theories of language and cognition?

There really are so many parallels between CDA and other work, that it is difficult to know where to start a list. For example, Fairclough & Wodak (1997: 259) talk of the 'widespread cynicism about the rhetoric of commodity advertising'. This theme, taken up in several text analyses elsewhere in Fairclough's work, is very reminiscent of the moral crusade against the vulgarising mass media and increasingly mechanised and capitalist society, which was carried out by F. R. Leavis and his colleagues in *Scrutiny* in the 1930s. The question arises as to how far CDA differs in methods and concepts from many types of literary criticism.

A large literature on stylistics debates whether interpretations of texts can be motivated from textual evidence. For example, Fish (1989) discusses the status of interpretations in literary theory and in the law. He shows the severe problems with formalist textual analyses, and argues that there are no unbiased interpretative judgements: all interpretations are done with an eye on the intentions of the author, within historical, professional and institutional contexts. A well known concept of Fish's, very relevant to concerns of CDA, but hardly discussed there, is the interpretative community.

Given CDA's emphasis on features of language use which are taken-for-granted, routine and naturalised, it is surprising that there is no discussion of the concept of the routine grounds of everyday activity which lie behind conversational analysis. But then there is little reference in CDA to the whole phenomenological tradition of thought within sociology, to Alfred Schutz for example, or to Berger & Luckmann's (1966) classic on 'the social construction of reality'.

The view that the common-sense world is always a rhetorical construction is familiar to linguists via Benjamin Lee Whorf's work. But, here again, CDA ignores a large literature on modern views of the language-thought relation within this tradition, including meticulous reassessments of Whorf by Lucy (1992) and by Gumperz & Levinson (1996). Whorf posed a still unresolved question: do diverse languages influence the habitual thought of their speakers? CDA shifts this question to different patterns of use within a single language. And in this form, the question is very widely posed by a range of thinkers in apparently rather different intellectual traditions.

Perhaps Fairclough might point out that most linguists don't read Foucault, whom he does discuss, on how discursive practices define human subjects. But then, notoriously, Foucault does not discuss methods of text analysis. And, in turn, Fairclough does not discuss work, explicitly inspired by Foucault, but with a much more concrete view of text analysis. For example, Said (1978) in his work on orientalism, studies a corpus of writings, to show textual traces of modes of thought. He cites repeated collocations of the word *oriental,* to show the presuppositions they convey. His detailed textual analyses make precise claims, which can be corroborated, and I have found in large corpora precisely some of the textual patterns which he identifies (Stubbs, 1996: 169).

There is much other work, with explicitly constructivist assumptions, which could be examined for its relevance to CDA. There is no reference to Searle's (1995) work on 'the construction of social reality': a careful analysis of the relation between language acts and institutional facts. Nor is there discussion of Lakoff & Johnson (1980) on how metaphors, fixed phrases and cliches influence habitual thought. They make explicit claims (p. 7) that 'a systematic way of talking' about a topic can be 'a portion of a conceptual network'. And there is much feminist linguistics (e.g. Cameron 1992) which refers sympathetically to Whorf.

Much of this huge body of work is not mentioned at all within CDA. Other work is referred to only fleetingly, and without any substantial evaluation of its relations to CDA. Indeed the whole tradition of 'critical theory', in the sense of work by the Frankfurt School, is referred to only occasionally. Fowler (1996: 4) makes a brief reference, and Fairclough & Wodak (1997: 260–61) provide brief summaries with no detailed explanation or direct comparison with CDA. Hammersley (1996) discusses this omission in detail.

Perhaps this is my main criticism. The position argued by CDA is not new at all. It has been debated since Plato and Aristotle. Plato was suspicious of the poets, and banished them from his Republic, lest they mislead people with their honeyed words. Aristotle also warned against the seductive appeal of rhetoric. The whole history of western thought could be written as this quarrel between philosophy and rhetoric: between the possibility of plain unvarnished truth and the insidious appeal of fine words; between the possibility of an independent truth and the inevitability of expressing things from a partisan point of view. Currently, we are in a phase in which the majority of social scientists believe in the impossibility of a neutral observation language, in which books such as Kuhn (1970) on paradigms of thought are among the most cited of all time, and in which a broad range of applied linguistic work has taken the 'critical' ideological turn in tune with the postmodernist Zeitgeist (Brumfit, 1996).

Given its own insistence on the positioning of the human subject by discourse, and on the inescapability of history (cf. Fowler, 1991b: 93 on 'discourse within history'), I find it surprising that CDA fails to examine in detail this broad historical tradition of thought. There are two ironies in CDA. First, it insists on interdisciplinary work, but underestimates just how widespread its central question has been across many disciplines and over many centuries. Second, it insists on the historical embedding of all language use, but does not recognise that it is posing the oldest question in philosophy.

My comments in the section above draw heavily on Fish (1989: especially 436–67 and 471–502), who provides a magisterial discussion of the problems of critical theory and of the history of rhetoric.

Proposals

I am now very aware of the following features of my own presentation. Criticisms are inherently negative. I have argued that there are certain kinds of circularity from which CDA simply cannot escape. However, some of the questions I have asked can be answered with empirical methods, which could strengthen CDA in various ways. I have proposed several criteria which it is quite possible to meet, and which have indeed been met in published work. The main ones are:

— ethnographic study of actual text-production (e.g. Bell, 1991)

— analysis of co-occurring linguistic features (e.g. Biber, 1988, 1995)

— comparison of texts and corpora, including diachronic and cross-language corpora (e.g. Krishnamurty, 1996; Stubbs, 1997)

— study of text dissemination and audience reception (e.g. Zipes, 1993, van Noppen, 1996).

In addition to studies of production and reception, the text analyses must, quite simply, be much more detailed. Analyses must be comparative: individual texts must be compared with each other and with data from corpora. Analyses must not be restricted to isolated data fragments: a much wider range of data must be sampled before generalisations are made about typical language use. And a much wider range of linguistic features must be studied, since varieties of language use are defined, not by individual features, but by clusters of co-occurring features: this entails the use of quantitative and probabilistic methods of text and corpus analysis.

In a short paper, I cannot provide detailed analyses of text and corpus data. However, I can set out the form of the argument, provide references to published studies, and outline how they might be related. For example, I have myself published work (Stubbs, 1994, 1996: 125–56), in which I have tried to show how CDA could be improved by comparative analysis of grammatical features across two long texts (two complete school textbooks) and a million word corpus. These comparative and intertextual analyses could be evaluated against the criteria I have discussed, to see if I have done any better than the work I am criticising.

I will outline two further case studies to show how individual texts could be compared with (1) other individual texts, against (2) an intertextual background of normative data from large historical and contemporary corpora. Such studies can also use socio-historical analysis of (3) the dissemination and reception of texts over time, and/or of (4) the discourse and beliefs of likely readers of the texts.

Case Study 1

Here is an example of how the use of a keyword in a text relates to its inter-textual background, and also to the political beliefs of intended readers.

As a starting point, but no more, I will comment on a text fragment, from an editorial in *Heritage Scotland* (1993: 10, 2), the magazine of the National Trust for Scotland. The title of the editorial, Who Cares?, is a play on words. The expression usually conveys extreme lack of interest. Here, the question is taken literally, and answered in the editorial. Here is the first paragraph.

> We regularly read newspaper headlines denouncing the 'moral sickness' within society. It is therefore important to all of us to know that there are caring organizations like the National Trust for Scotland, which not only preserves and protects buildings, landscape and inanimate objects, but also cares for the people and the communities at its properties.

The lexeme CARE has acquired political implications in contemporary British English, as in recurring phrases such as health care, care in the community and caring society. One might say, rather cynically, that such uses signal an uncaring society, conceived of mainly in economic terms. However, the only way to substantiate such rough observations is to use a corpus. In other work (Stubbs, 1996: 184; 1997), I have studied changes in the meaning and grammar of CARE, by looking at over 40,000 examples in large diachronic and contemporary corpora. Since around 1900, the noun *care* has undergone a change from predominantly personal uses (to take care of someone) to very frequent institutional uses (child care). The form *caring* occurs only from the 1960s as a prenominal adjective (a caring society, the caring professions). And the word *carer* appears only in the late 1970s. This is precisely the kind of changing discourse which CDA identifies, but does not document diachronically or quantitatively. (For an independent corpus study of CARE, see Johnson, 1993).

CDA also emphasises that changes in British English are part of much wider European or even global changes. Again, such claims could be documented only by corpus studies. In a smaller study (Stubbs 1997), I have investigated some of the changes in the German word PFLEGEN (= CARE) across several thousand examples from a German-language corpus, to show that it is also a keyword in contemporary German society (e.g. Pflegeberufe = caring professions).

Finally, as part of a study of how contemporary Scotland is represented in the media, especially in tourist advertising, McCrone *et al.* (1995) analyse the membership of the National Trust for Scotland, the intended audience for the editorial text, its social class make-up and the political beliefs of its members, and also provide detailed examples of their discourse, collected in interviews about their views on the concept of 'heritage'.

Concretely, such a study could relate analyses of:

— an individual text about 'caring for the environment'

— recent changes in connotations of the word CARE in the UK – wider, cross-language changes in this semantic field

— the target group of readers and their language.

Case Study 2

A basic criterion is that work must be comparative. In a socially very influential case of the same story told from different ideological points of view, Zipes (1993) has published 38 English-language versions, from the 1600s to the present, of Little Red Riding Hood. He discusses the textual and social history of the story, including versions by Perrault (late 1600s) and the Brothers Grimm (early 1800s), which had huge circulations and a large influence in the education of children. He analyses the techniques and discursive strategies by which violence is represented, both in the texts and in their accompanying illustrations, and also in the frequent intertextual references in contemporary advertising and films. In short, he discusses the adaptation, dissemination and reception of the most widespread and notorious fairy tale in the western world, with its themes of adolescence and obedience, and how it has been used to control gender roles and social norms. Such a case study illustrates in textual detail Foucault's (1980) theses on social control, sex and education.

A keyword in many of the versions is LITTLE. In other work (Stubbs 1995, 1997), I have studied 300,000 occurrences of the adjectives LITTLE, SMALL, BIG and LARGE, to show that they occur in largely complementary distribution, and have quite different uses and collocates. In particular, LITTLE has strong cultural connotations. The following facts are very simple, but not explicitly presented in any dictionary I have found. In a 200-million word corpus of contemporary English, the most common noun to co-occur with LITTLE is GIRL. The phrase *little girl(s)* is nearly 20 times as common as *small girl(s),* whereas the phrase *little boy(s)* is only twice as common as *small boy(s).* The combination *little man* is almost always pejorative, as in *ridiculous little man.* Briefly, LITTLE frequently has strong connotative meanings of 'cute and cuddly', or alternatively pejorative meanings. The combination of +female and +pejorative features is a well known phenomenon. (See Baker & Freebody, 1989 for an independent analysis of the 'cuddle' component of its meaning in a corpus of children's readers.) Such data provide a clear intertextual explanation of why the word LITTLE has the connotations it does in the phrase Little Red Riding Hood (also Little Miss Muffet, Little Jack Horner).

In summary, it would be possible to combine analyses of:

— the historical development of different versions of a text

— its dissemination: publication history, sales, etc.

— its use in social control and education

— its intertextual background (e.g. connotations of keywords).

CDA does not provide any criteria for selecting texts for analysis. Its methods do not distinguish between texts which have a restricted audience, and texts which have been adapted, read and retold uncountable times, learned by heart, and constantly alluded to over centuries. Tales such as Little Red Riding Hood have been studied in detail by many commentators, and Zipes is, of course, not working within CDA. A test for CDA would be: Can it add anything to such commentaries? Is it any advance on literary critical methods?

Conclusions

Such examples show that it is not unduly difficult to carry out studies which would meet at least some of the criteria I have proposed. Would it however be worthwhile? If you are interested in persuasion, in convincing people that ideas are often manipulated by uses of language, then you might feel that such studies, including analyses of millions of words of corpus data, are overkill. They seem to show in detail what is really rather obvious. However, although the facts about CARE and LITTLE may seem obvious in retrospect, they are discoverable only via work on large corpora, and are not open to unaided introspection. And, if you are interested in a systematic and thoroughly documented study of cultural transmission, reproduction and change, then such studies are necessary.

But in either case, you would have to recognise that the interpretations are ultimately circular. If you come to agree that CARE (as in *caring society*) is a weasel-word in contemporary Britain, or that Little Red Riding Hood is not the innocent tale you once thought it was, then these are not objective findings, but personal convictions. I happen to have been convinced of them, and it feels as though this was a free and rational choice. Both Fairclough (1995a: 231) and Fowler (1996: 4) see 'emancipation' as 'the founding motivation for critical analysis'. (See also Fairclough & Wodak, 1997: 259.) But Fish (1989: 467) reveals this as an illusion, and points out that:

> It is because history is inescapable that every historical moment – that is, every moment – feels so much like an escape.

At the beginning of the article, I expressed the hope that my criticisms would be taken in a positive spirit. CDA has set an important agenda, of potentially very considerable social significance. It is therefore important that both the details, and also the central logic of the argument, are as carefully worked out as possible.

Acknowledgements

For comments on previous drafts, I am grateful to Wolfram Bublitz, Joanna Channell, Norman Fairclough, Andrea Gerbig, Anthony Johnson and Gabi Keck.

These colleagues do not necessarily agree with my arguments, and Norman Fairclough certainly wishes to reserve his position.

References

Baker, C. and Freebody, P. (1989) *Children's First School Books*. Oxford: Blackwell.

Bell, A. (1991) *The Language of News Media*. Oxford: Blackwell.

Berger, P. and Luckmann, T. (1966) *The Social Construction of Reality*. London: Allen Lane.

Biber, D. (1988) *Variation across Speech and Writing*. Cambridge: Cambridge University Press.

— (1995) *Dimensions of Register Variation*. Cambridge: Cambridge University Press.

Brumfit, C. (1996) Theoretical practice: Applied linguistics as pure and practical science. Paper read to AILA Congress, Jyväskylä.

Caldas-Coulthard, R. and Coulthard, M. (eds) (1996) *Texts and Practices: Readings in critical discourse analysis*. London: Routledge.

Cameron, D. (1992) *Feminism and Linguistic Theory*. 2nd edn. London: Macmillan.

Coseriu, E. (1988) *Sprachkompetenz*. Tübingen: Francke.

Ehlich, K. (ed.) (1989) *Sprache im Faschismus*. Frankfurt: Suhrkamp.

Fairclough, N. (1989) *Language and Power*. London: Longman.

— (1992) *Discourse and Social Change*. Oxford: Polity.

— (1995a) *Critical Discourse Analysis*. London: Longman.

— (1995b) *Media Discourse*. London: Arnold.

Fairclough, N. and Mauranen, A. (in press) The conversationalization of political discourse: a comparative view. In J. Blommaert (ed.) On political linguistics. *Belgian Journal of Applied Linguistics*.

Fairclough, N. and Wodak, R. (1997) Critical discourse analysis. In T. A. van Dijk (ed.) *Introduction to Discourse Analysis*. Newbury Park: Sage.

Fish, S. (1989) *Doing What Comes Naturally*. Oxford: Clarendon.

Foucault, M. (1980) *Power/Knowledge*. C. Gordon (ed.). London: Harvester.

Fowler, R. (1991a) *Language in the News*. London: Routledge.

— (1991b) Critical linguistics. In K. Malmkjaer (ed.) *The Linguistics Encyclopedia* (pp. 89–93). London: Routledge.

— (1996) On critical linguistics. In R. Caldas-Coulthard and M. Coulthard (eds) *Texts and Practices: Readings in critical discourse analysis* (pp. 3–14). London: Routledge.

Gumperz, J. J. and S. C. Levinson, S. C. (eds) (1996) *Rethinking Linguistic Relativity*. Cambridge: Cambridge University Press.

Hammersley, M. (1996) On the foundations of critical discourse analysis. *Occasional Paper 42*. Centre for Language in Education, University of Southampton.

Hodge, R. and Kress, G. (1988) *Social Semiotics*. Oxford: Polity.

— (1993) *Language as Ideology*. 2nd edn. London: Routledge.

Johnson, A. (1993) The use of informal interviews in the study of 'care' in family life. PhD thesis, University of Nottingham.

Kress, G. (1990) Critical discourse analysis. *Annual Review of Applied Linguistics* 11, 84–99.

Krishnamurty, R. (1996) Ethnic, racial and tribal: The language of racism? In R. Caldas-Coulthard and M. Coulthard (eds) *Texts and Practices: Readings in critical discourse analysis* (pp. 129–49). London: Routledge.

Kuhn, T. (1970) *The Structure of Scientific Revolutions*. Chicago: Chicago University Press.

Lakoff, G. and Johnson, M. (1980) *Metaphors We Live By*. Chicago: University of Chicago Press.

Lucy, J. A. (1992) *Language Diversity and Thought*. Cambridge: Cambridge University Press.

McCrone, D., Morris, A. and Kiely, R. (1995) *Scotland – the Brand*. Edinburgh: Edinburgh University Press.

Meinhof, U. and Richardson, K. (eds) (1994) *Text, Discourse and Context*. London: Longman.

Richardson, K. (1987) Critical linguistics and textual diagnosis. *Text* 7, 2, 145–63.

Said, E. (1978) *Orientalism*. London: Routledge & Kegan Paul.

Searle, J. (1995) *The Construction of Social Reality*. London: Allen Lane.

Sharrock, W. W. and Anderson, D. C. (1981) Language, thought and reality, again. *Sociology* 15, 287–93.

Stubbs, M. (1994) Grammar, text and ideology. *Applied Linguistics* 15, 2, 201–23.

— (1995) Collocations and cultural connotations of common words. *Linguistics and Education* 7, 4, 379–90.

— (1996) *Text and Corpus Analysis*. Oxford: Blackwell.

— (1997, in press) 'Eine Sprache idiomatisch sprechen': Computer, Korpora, Kommunikative Kompetenz und Kultur. In K. J. Matheier (ed.) *Norm und Variation*. Frankfurt: Lang.

van Noppen, J-P. (1996) *Critical Theolinguistics: Methodism, its discourse and its work ethic*. University of Duisburg: LAUD Working Papers.

Widdowson, H. G. (1995a) Discourse analysis: a critical view. *Language and Literature* 4, 3, 157–72.

— (1995b) Review of Fairclough Discourse and Social Change, *Applied Linguistics* 16, 4, 510–16.

— (1996) Discourse and interpretation: conjectures and refutations [= Reply to Fairclough 1996]. *Language and Literature* 5, 1, 57–69.

Wodak, R. (1996) The genesis of racist discourse in Austria since 1989. In R. Caldas-Coulthard and M. Coulthard (eds) *Texts and Practices: Readings in critical discourse analysis* (pp. 107–28). London: Routledge.

Zipes, J. (ed.) (1993) *The Trials and Tribulations of Little Red Riding Hood*. 2nd edn. London: Routledge.

Contributors

J. Charles Alderson is Professor of Linguistics and English Language Education in the Department of Linguistics and Modern English Language and was Head of Department from 1994 to 1997. His main research interests are in language testing, evaluation of second language education, and processing second and foreign languages.

Jonathan Charteris-Black works as a lecturer at the University of Surrey where he teaches on the MA in Linguistics (TESOL) distance learning programme run by the English Language Institute. He learnt Moroccan Arabic and Malay while working as a teacher of English in Morocco and Brunei. His published research is concerned with the interrelationships of language and culture as revealed by contrastive rhetoric and by phraseological systems. In SLA contexts, these impinge on the acquisition of L2 English writing and L2 speaking respectively.

Nick Ellis is Reader in Psychology at the University of Wales, Bangor. His research interests include: first, second and foreign language acquisition; connectionist and emergentist accounts of cognitive development; imagery; memory; reading, spelling and dyslexia; semantics; the role of consciousness in learning.

Tom Hales is a Senior Tutor in the Centre for Applied Language Studies in the University of Wales, Swansea. This follows spells as a commercial programmer and teaching overseas. In addition to the teaching of undergraduate linguistics, his research work has led increasingly to an interest in corpus analysis and in particular the analysis of specialised texts. Recent publications have concentrated on the analysis of financial corpora.

David Malvern joined the University of Reading as a Research Officer with the Schools Council Sixth Form Mathematics Project. Since then he has been seconded to the Royal Society, has been a Visiting Professor at McGill University, an international consultant for the European Community and the Overseas Development Administration, and is now Senior Lecturer in Science and Mathematics Education. He has directed a joint project with Berkshire LEA on Language in Primary Mathematics and has extensive experience of students learning science through the medium of a second language.

James Milton has been Director of the Centre for Applied Language Studies in the University of Wales, Swansea since 1986. Current areas of interest include vocabulary acquisition and the nature of technical text. This has led not only to research publications but to the writing of tailor-made technical glossaries and commercial vocabulary teaching materials.

Akiko Okamura is a lecturer in Japanese in the Language Centre at Newcastle University. She is currently working on the roles of culture and language in the scientific discourse for her PhD.

Brian Richards taught languages in South Wales and Germany before joining the Bristol Study of Language Development and completing a PhD on children's language development in 1987. He is currently Senior Lecturer and Research Co-ordinator in the Department of Arts and Humanities in Education at the University of Reading, and is Associate Editor of the *Journal of Child Language*. He is author of *Language Development and Individual Differences* (1990) and co-editor of *Input and Interaction in Language Acquisition* (with Clare Gallaway, 1994).

Ann Ryan has been a lecturer in the Centre for Applied Language Studies at the University of Wales, Swansea, since 1986. She teaches on an undergraduate course in English Language as well as training teachers for teaching English as a foreign language. Her research interests are in the field of second language acquisition and dyslexia.

Michael Stubbs has been Professor of English Linguistics at the University of Trier, Germany, since 1990. He was previously Professor of English in Education at the Institute of Education, University of London (1985–90), Lecturer in Linguistics, University of Nottingham (1974–85), and Visiting Professor at the University of Tübingen (1985); he is Senior Honorary Research Fellow at the University of Birmingham. He has been (1988–91) chair of BAAL. His most recent book is *Text and Corpus Analysis* (1996, Blackwell).

Alison Wray has been Assistant Director of the Wales Applied Language Research Unit in CALS, University of Wales, Swansea since 1996, before which she was a Senior Lecturer in linguistics at the University of Ripon & York St. John. She has two major research areas: the nature and status of *formulae* (multi-word units) in language processing, and the pronunciation of English, French and Latin in early music.